A Misplaced Priority

A Misplaced Priority

A BIBLICAL VISION OF FOLLOWERSHIP

Ubong Ntewo

Edited by

Chima Ikonne

Endorsements

Misplaced Priority is a call to the church to prioritize raising up believers who will live out biblical followership. Ubi does a masterful job helping his readers understand that followership, not leadership, should be the preeminent virtue and discipline of any movement that desires to be effective and lasting.

-   *Rev. Alan D. Scott, Lead Pastor, Oakhill Baptist Church. Evansville, Indiana.*

Ubi's reminder of the Biblical mandate to followership is a wake-up call to the leadership-crazed mindset that has plagued the western church for decades. It is a fresh call to be an imitator of Christ and a must read for all who truly desire to understand the holiness of God.

– *Prince Samuel. Lead Pastor, Bethel Church. Evansville, Indiana.*

A Misplaced Priority is eye opening and challenging. It created a shift in perspective of my view of Biblical leadership. A Misplaced Priority is a must read for both those in leadership and for those under leadership. With the increased attention leadership is being given among our youth, A Misplaced Priority is a countercultural message that our high school and college students need to hear.

- *Jason Brand. Multi-Area Director, Fellowship of Christian Athletes. Southwest Indiana*

Wow! I just finished reading, A Misplaced Priority, in which Ubi challenges the concept of "leadership only" by reminding us of God's call to followership also. Truth be told, we all believe in this concept, but many times do not model it. He speaks of recognizing leadership and followership as opposite sides of the Christian discipleship coin.

Working face to face with young, emerging leaders I personally have seen the conflict in their lives, to live their calling and not be crushed by the leadership only way of thinking.

After reading this I will adopt his phrase "Follow the good, Lead to the good."

- *Lloyd Ziegler. Founder, Masters Commission.*

DEDICATION

To my king, Jesus the glorious, chosen and empowered by God Almighty. Take from me this paltry offering and make of it a miracle.

To the church, beautiful bride of Jesus. May you display more and more the glory of your king.

Table of Contents

X

Preface

This book is a product of scripture bearing down on my personal experiences and observations of current church culture. Although, research evidence exists in support of the claims made in this book, I chose not to rely on them but instead to appeal to scripture and the common experiences of the reader. I cannot imagine anyone would deny that as a society, we have become increasingly obsessed with leadership while simultaneously developing an aversion to followership.

A Misplaced Priority is an attempt to offer a bird's-eye view of what I believe to be the biblical teaching on the followership-leadership dynamic. Therefore, its brief handling of a subject that deserves further exploration and interaction. The questions at the end of every chapter should be used to assist with delving deeper into the books content and subject matter.

Furthermore, I have attempted to arrange the material loosely while still maintaining a logically cohesive form. First, I explore the meaning and nature of followership in relationship to God. Next, the relationship between followership and leadership is explored. Here, I lay out the case for the greatness and importance of followership over leadership. Third, I argue that one must first be able to follow their neighbor before they can follow God. The final section explores characteristics of godly, wise and responsible followership. This list of characteristics is by no means exhaustive. However, I believe they serve as the building blocks for the followership taught by scripture and extolled by God.

In referencing this discourse as an exploration of the followership-leadership dynamic, I do not attempt to give equal ink to the discipline of leadership. My goal here is to show that its relationship to followership is similar to that of a child to its parent. The child's survival and growth into responsible adulthood, depends in large part, on the healthy functioning and presence of the parent.

Acknowledgements

My dearest friend and wife, I truly believe that without you I could not have written this book. It was you who planted the seeds of the writer in me. I remember that on several occasions after proof reading my college papers, you urged me to write for the edification of the church. Thank you for encouraging and allowing me the time and space to follow my call. I love you more with each passing day.

To my professors at Indiana Wesleyan University, thank you for challenging me to pursue writing as a call and career. The continued prompting from such esteemed scholars and lovers of God served as a much-needed nourishment.

Thanks to all those who read and critiqued the manuscript, your feedback was priceless. Austin

Maxheimer and Jason Brand, thank you for challenging me to clarify the relationship between followership and the Gospel.

To the leaders and alumni of Evansville Masters Commission who answered my appeal for feedback, thank you. Leigh Ann, Cassie, Zach and Josh, just having you respond was such an affirmation of your love and support. Pam, you rock! Thanks for always challenging and pushing us to be, "Jesus with skin on." Pastors Z and Chris, in many ways, I am a product of your faithfulness. Thank you for being a model to so many.

To Tracee, Britney and the baristas of Starbucks on Green River (Store #9759) and Burkhardt (Store #8955), thank you for creating a welcoming and friendly space to write, think and chill. Dan and Emily, it was a pleasure studying alongside you.

Albert and Summerly Sanchez of Eternal Life, thank you for designing the book cover.

Glory, honor and praise be to the one true and only God, for in his love, he chose us, to live victorious in Christ Jesus.

Introduction

The Good News of Jesus Christ is both a command and an invitation to humanity. In it, the creator and sustainer of all things calls us to recognize and trust Jesus Christ as our sovereign king and savior.

God promises that those of us who respond positively to this command-invitation will be saved from the power, consequence and penalty of sin. Sin is rebellion against God. It is all that misses the mark of God's rightness. The penalty of sin is unending torment and separation from God in eternity. However, we experience the power and consequences of sin even now, lust, destruction, desolation, loss and death. These are the immediate out workings of sin and those who refuse to acknowledge God, immerse in it, every day.

In addition to God's promise of salvation from sin is his promise to usher the obedient into eternal life. To have this life, is to have fellowship with God. It is the favorable experience of living daily in his presence and participating in his Life. This experience is possessed even now by those who acknowledge and trust Jesus to be the sovereign king and savior of all. This is the condition of the Christian in this world and moment, to experience an ever-intensifying joy, peace and righteousness through faith in Jesus. It is to grow into what he was when he lived on earth. This is the Gospel, a command-invitation from God that is too good to be true, and yet is.

The command-invitation to recognize and trust Jesus is to be fleshed out in following Him. Thus, his repeated exhortation as found in scripture "follow me". Basically, the experience of salvation from condemnation and participation in eternal life is greatly affected by the manner in which Jesus is followed. If followed noncommittally or reservedly, the experience of salvation and new life, in the here and now, is hardly perceptively. On the other hand, an all-out pursuit of Jesus Christ will result in an experience of the spirit-filled life and an expression of the kingdom of God in day to day moments.

In a culture where followership is at best ignored and at worst despised, how does one learn to follow? Or muster the desire and strength to follow? In a society where leadership is intensely coveted and used to measure one's worth and value, the virtue of followership is perceived as a vice and weakness. Parents tell their children to lead and not follow. Organizations and businesses determine eligibility on the basis of the leadership qualities possessed by their desperate candidates. Institutions of learning offer degrees and certification courses at the highest levels on leadership. Meanwhile, followership is not even considered a discipline or skill. Yet God rest his eternal and glorious promises on the mandate to follow Jesus. God's actions demand that we give serious attention to understanding the nature of followership and its importance for the flourishing of the church, the Christian and society at large.

A Misplaced Priority seeks to serves as a starter guide to a scriptural exploration of the nature and importance of followership. In scripture, we find that followership is the source and sustainer of Stewardship, of which leadership is a part. As such followership is found to require great discipline, strength and discernment. Following is not a task to be entered lightly nor is it a haphazard act. Godly followership is purposeful and dynamic. As you read the pages of this book, I pray that you come to understand that followership, like leadership is a capacity that must be honed into a skill and discipline. Furthermore, I pray that you become convinced of its primacy over leadership, for it is the foundation upon which true leadership is built. And the rock in which leadership finds shelter, protection and nourishment. I expect you will come to see that to follow responsibly and godly is to discover the path to your best and truest self.

Following the Leadership Crowd

My wife and I have three kids, ages nine, eight and seven. As you can imagine raising them has been quite the adventure. Heather and I were married eleven years ago and from the outset committed to raising our kids to love God by trusting and obeying Jesus Christ. Coupled with this lofty ambition is the desire that our kids grow up to love one another and serve the church with their gifts according to God's will. Up to this point all of our parenting has been geared in one form or another towards these goals. So, imagine my dismay at discovering I was deeply irritated because my youngest child tended to easily give in to the desires of the other kids in our neighborhood. After all, his inclination to deference did not appear to

1

negatively affect the goal of our parenting. Initially, I thought I was simply being over protective. I was worried that these kids might be a negative influence on "my little angels." And for good reason, not too long ago we found out that, Michael, a kid in the neighborhood had advised them to go against our instructions. We'd told them not to go to the house of a neighbor without first obtaining our permission. Michael, "the bad kid," urged them to go over to the neighbor's assuring them we wouldn't find out and even if we did, would do nothing about it. Surely then, my protective instincts must have been the reason for this irritation. However, successive bouts of irritation at my son's continuing attitude of deference even to suggestions from his peers to act in ways I considered right and commendable, hinted at something more.

Over the years, I have developed the discipline of using the Bible as my standard for regular self-examination. By the grace of God this practice continues to pay huge dividends aiding in growing my faith and devotion to Jesus. It has served to ensure that I am honest with both myself and the Lord. Additionally, it has kept me grounded and helped in curbing many of my weaknesses and vices. Curtailing them from leading to irreparable damage in my relationships and service to the church. Interestingly, prayerful examination and reflection on this persistent irritation yielded nothing. I was unable to fathom its source or reason for being. I remained in this state of perplexity and irritation, until one faithful Sunday. I was slated to serve in the kids' department of a church I had recently joined as their Family Pastor. At the kids- check-in station that morning, a mother was dropping of her child. Before kissing her little girl good-bye, she looked right into her eyes and said, "Remember, you are a leader." How ridiculous! I thought. Here was a child barely five years of age, already being burdened with the idea of defining and taking her place in society, as a leader. While criticizing this mother's actions in my mind, a light bulb came on. The only difference between this mother and I was that she had clearly verbalized what I unconsciously but earnestly desired for all my kids! Like her, I wanted my children to grow up to be leaders. I was irritated and disturbed by the fact that my younger son was turning out to be a follower and not the leader of his peers, I intensely wanted him to become.

As a society, we have created a culture that celebrates and adores leaders and leadership. This is evident in the plethora of books and conferences that focus on this single topic. We are consistently bombarded with principles and lessons urging us to become more effective leaders. Frequently, we find that one's chances at being admitted into a college or even hired for a job, hinge on whether or not they are perceived as leaders or individuals who display leadership qualities. Obviously, this favorable stance towards leadership has led to a despising of followership. Yes, followership is now passé. To be a follower is to be blind, indecisive and weak. For some, to be a follower is to be a failure. Given this state of affairs, it should have been little surprise that I desperately wanted my kids to be leaders. After all, to be a success in today's world is to be a leader. I was shocked and bothered that I so intensely desired for my kids, as well as myself, to be leaders. But I was more disturbed at the fact that I had unconsciously embraced this dual attitude of celebrating and coveting leadership, while despising followership.

This awakening led me to a thorough examination of my attitude towards the leadership-followership relationship. But even more, it caused me to ponder the nature and relevance of followership. I was pretty familiar with leadership, its importance and effect on any society or organization. I had gained this understanding of leadership from life experience, vocational school, college classes, leadership seminars and books. On the other hand, I realized I knew next to nothing about followership. What exactly is followership? Does it deserve the bad reputation it has gained? Can society afford to treat followership as a passing and outmoded concept or discipline? And what effects, if any, does followership have on society? Suffice to say, leadership is necessary to the successful functioning of any organization and society. Those who desire to be leaders should be commended, if they are driven by a selfless passion to serve the collective in fulfilling its God given mission. In this light, our celebration and focus on leadership is not inherently wrong. It is only problematic due to its excessive and covetous nature. But what about "followership," is that even a word? In a number of conversations, I have been asked that question. I must confess, initially I was not sure myself. I simply assumed that since leadership was a word, it would not be wrong to pen "followership." Imagine my disappointment at finding it in a dictionary. My ignorance and that of so many others, confirms as fact that we have relegated followership to a point of near extinction. Currently, it exists only because it must. It is something we do under compulsion and out of necessity. If not for this, followership would be nothing more than a word that simply exist in our dictionaries! But of course, followership must exist. After all, the very presence and reality of leaders implies that someone is following. The issue is the societal stigma associated with followership. The ignominy associated with followership ensures that it is done passively, unwillingly and without thought or pride. What follows are truths about followership gleaned from a careful survey of scripture and a superimposition of its teachings on my experiences and observations of society.

A Misplaced Priority

Questions (Following the Leadership Crowd)

1. Do you believe our culture currently despises followership?
   a. If yes, share your observations of our aversion to follow?
   b. If no, what do you believe is the society's current attitude towards followership?

2. Did your parents ever tell to be a leader not a follower, or something similar?
   a. What do you think were their reasons for this instruction?

3. Can you relate to the author's frustration at his child's tendency to follow others?

COMPLYING WITH JESUS

A dictionary definition holds a follower to be anyone who acts in accordance with the directions of another. Later on, I will address the concept of followership existing in two forms, compliance and imitation. Working with this simple definition for now, we might say that everyone is a follower in one sense or another. For example, most of us act in accordance with the directions of our supervisors at places of work; teachers at school and parents at home. In cases such as these, the act of following is initiated and sustained by the presence of an immediate outside influence or motivation, e.g. a paycheck. The absence of this immediate influence or motivation would quickly result in the termination of our followership. In speaking of one as a follower, I am referring more to their natural inclination or voluntary exercise. In other words, these are people naturally predisposed to complying with the directives and desires of others. There is little to no exertion of an immediate outside influence or motivation to garner the compliance of such persons. Thus, followers are people who are comfortable and fulfilled when acting in compliance with the instructions and opinions of other people. There are many people who follow but find neither comfort nor fulfillment in the exercise. The impetus and motivation of their compliance lies solely in the presence of an external influence. While they may find a reward or benefit for following, followership itself is never the end goal. In present society the overwhelming majority consist of such persons. This is due in large part to our obsession with and excessive focus on leadership. To most of society, leadership is perceived as a moral mandate and virtue. As a result, we tend to find fulfillment and satisfaction in the very act of leading, while following elicits feelings of frustration and angst.

Bringing this definition to bear on our relationship with the Lord reveals that we are not to be people who simply follow Jesus' instructions. The followership that Jesus calls us to is not one filled with vexation and anxiety. And though, it offers both immediate and future reward, we find these are neither its motivation nor bases. The foundation and impetus for following Jesus, are his sacrificial love and confirmed identity as the way to God, the truth of God and the life of God. Followership of this sort calls us to be people who at our core are comforted, strengthened and fulfilled in going after Jesus. This kind of following requires a change in one's nature, motivations and character. Complying with Jesus' commands and teachings should become more automatic, more comfortable and more fulfilling as we grow in faith. Instead of cringing from obedience at the prospect of the shame and suffering we will receive from the hands of others, we should be spurred on by the sense of joy and victory we will experience in our hearts from the hands of the Holy Spirit. It should also be noted that Christian following is not due to an exertion from outside us but as a result of the consistent and transformative work of the Holy Spirit within us. The Spirit of Christ is present in us as teacher, guide, comforter and friend. It is the

Holy Spirit who consistently gives us the assurance of Jesus' love; it is the Holy Spirit who convinces and gives us certainty of Jesus' identity as the Son of God and Savior from God. One work of the Holy Spirit in the life of every true Christian is his act of transforming the crucifixion of Christ from a static event in history to a dynamic reality that captivates our hearts and minds. Here we catch a glimpse of what God means when he says, that his Holy Spirit pours out his love within our hearts (Romans 5.5).

In speaking of following Jesus as automatic, I mean that our compliance should gradually become more reflexive as the days go by, this is growing in the Spirit. Following Jesus' life, commands and teachings, must always be an active endeavor in the Christian's life, but at the same time it should also grow more and more into an impulse that dominates the unconscious aspects of our being. This becomes possible when we begin familiarizing and immersing ourselves in his life and words. Basically, successfully following Jesus by act and reflex requires that we consistently read, study and meditate on his life as revealed in scripture.

Jesus declares that his words are spiritual, meaning that the Holy Spirit gives understanding and makes them effective in one's life. So, Bible immersion must be understood as the first and prime act of communion and surrender to Jesus' spirit. The Holy Spirit begins to simultaneously illumine the truth to my mind and heart, while making my desires and will consistent with it. True followership begins, continues and ends in scripture immersion.

As the Holy Spirit's work on our desires progresses, we discover that following Jesus' commands and teachings are not burdensome, instead they are comfortable and affirming. This presence of ease in obedience, signals the continuing change in our nature from carnal to spiritual. It is important to remember that though we may experience ease of obedience in one area of our lives, we will suffer difficulty in others. This indicates that there are still attitudes, ambitions and motives that we have not subjected to the will of God or brought his Word to act on. Also, the presence of a struggle with temptation is a simple but clear indicator of the fact that we are growing in holiness. Thus far, we have not arrived at perfection; we are not yet a complete or absolute expression of the image and character of Jesus Christ. While keeping us humbly on our knees, this truth also acts to restrain us from judging others to quickly. When judgment is necessary (*compare* John 7.24, Luke 12.57 to Luke 6.37, Matthew 7.1), an awareness of this truth should serve as a compulsion to the exercise of mercy. Finally, the difficulty of active compliance to Jesus ensures that we keep vigilant watch to maintain the subjection of our carnal nature, the ever-present enemy of us and our loving Father. Thus, on this side of eternity, we find following Jesus to be an unrelenting exercise requiring great effort and great trust. As it continues, we experience the power of Christ, dominating and consuming every aspect of our being.

Jesus referred to following God as his food (John 4.34) and the same must be true for you, if you are genuinely Christian. The new spiritual nature we have from God through faith in Christ is sustained, strengthened and refreshed in followership. This is why no Christian can remain in sin (1Jn 3.9). At its core sin is rebellion against God, his character and commands. It is the failure to follow Him and what he stands for. If following God is our food and nourishment, failure to follow him is equivalent to starving one's self and results in a weakening of our new spiritual life. Prolonged periods of abstinence from nourishment eventually result in our bodies revolting by signaling the need for sustenance with intense and prolonged pangs of pain. The same is true for the Christian who habitually walks in sin. We experience deep sorrow and anguish at our hardness of heart and distance from God. These painful experiences can only be terminated when we in repentance turn to God and recommit ourselves to living in obedience to his will as revealed in scripture. This holy discomfort and dissatisfaction are not only experienced when we do things that we ought not to, it also occurs when we fail to do things that we ought to do. This is to say, there is such a thing as passive disobedience. It takes place, when, we simply neglect to do those things that Jesus commands, as opposed to blatantly acting contrary to them. One area of the Christian life in which passive disobedience appears most prominently is in discipleship (evangelism and mentorship). Scripture teaches that it is the duty of every Christian to actively engage in the making of disciples. This is a process scripture shows Jesus to have been deeply committed to and invested in, while he lived on earth. An essential aspect of making disciples is telling non-believers about God's gracious act of salvation through Christ Jesus. However, too many of us choose not to get involved in this venture. What we fail to recognize is that our neglecting to tell the non-believer the gospel gives rise to a great degree of holy dissatisfaction in our lives. It is possible that you sense a lack of love or compassion for others and are perturbed that as a Christian you would feel this way. You want to love people but have no clue what do. You can start with praying and then sharing the message of God's immeasurable love with them. I have often been in conversations with fellow Christians where dissatisfaction at the lack of passion and spiritual vitality in many churches is mourned. It seems to me that the presence of new converts in the local church typically creates excitement and vitality. Their excitement, passion and inquisitiveness into their newfound faith and experience are always infectious. Talk less of their bold and sometimes reckless passion that requires the more seasoned to step into their roles as mentors. More times than not, their boldness and vibrant faith challenges those of us who have done "church" for several years. Churches and individuals experiencing revival of this nature are not simply living an exciting moment, they are also experiencing the satisfaction and blessing that comes from following, which is feeding on God's word. Finding satisfaction in following Jesus is probably the clearest proof that we have become people with a radically new nature. Just as we must eat food for the sustenance and nourishment of our natural bodies, we must follow God for the sustenance and vitality of our renewed nature. Picturing following Jesus as eating food, allows us to see the strangeness and counter-productivity of our reluctance to comply with him. This picture also reveals the destructive nature of any impulses that resist the desire to obey. To not follow Jesus is akin to committing spiritual suicide by slow and torturous starvation. One may initially have a euphoric experience but if they continue to neglect eating, they will eventually die. The sense of euphoria one experiences when they go for an extended period of time without eating may be likened to the initial sense of carnal freedom and excitement experienced when we turn from obeying Christ. However, persisting in this path will only end in pain, sorrow and ultimately destruction.

Questions (Complying with Jesus)

1. In what areas of your life do you find compliance with Jesus to be reflexive or automatic?
   a. How have you developed this reflexive instinct to comply?

2. In what aspects of your life is following Jesus an active endeavor?
   a. What specific actions are you taking?

3. In what specific ways do you find complying with Jesus to be nourishing?

IMITATING JESUS

So far, we have addressed followership as the disposition to, or act of, compliance with the directives of others, specifically Jesus. However, followership is also defined as the disposition to, or act of, imitating others. Basically, followership is both compliance and imitation. When these two forms are juxtaposed against each other, compliance is seen to be a lower form of followership for the Christian. Followership is manifested in a higher form as a disposition to imitate. It cannot be overstated that the imitation of Christ is of a higher and more intimate nature than is compliance to His commands. In observing the Gospel message, we discover that the invitation and command to comply with Christ's teachings precedes the call to imitate his life. As a matter fact, one could say that an essential aspect of the good news of salvation is that through faith in Jesus, we can now be brought into the experience of fellowship with God. We experience this fellowship when the relationship Jesus Christ has with the Father is both replicated by God an imitated by us. The experience of this replication and imitation is contingent on our obedience to the Gospel's command to believe and repent. Thus, compliance to Christ's command is a prerequisite for entrance into the replication of his life in us. It is obvious that a major problem faced by many Christians is that we view our faith solely as a journey from one successive act of compliance to another. In this light, living in Christ is not very different from living according to the Law. The major difference is that even though we feel remorse when we fail to comply with a certain command, we are not condemned because Christ has paid the price for our failure to move to the next step of compliance. The fact is that the Christian is called to a replicating of Christ's life in theirs through a work of imitation superintended and empowered by the person of the Holy Spirit. It is not an ongoing endeavor to fulfill the dictates of the law.

Compliance is a lower form because its goal is to make us imitators and replicas of Christ. In one sense, compliance serves in a catalytic and initiatory capacity. It initiates us into the ongoing process of the imitation of Christ. We find an illustration of this fact in the conclusion of Matthew 5 where Jesus lays down instructions and teachings for how we should live. He concludes by stating that we are to be perfect, as God is perfect. In Luke 6.20-36, He repeats the same process. Instructions and commands to be followed are laid out with the end goal of these instructions being the imitation of God and the replication of Jesus' life in ours.

Imitation followership is not only a higher form because it is the overarching purpose of compliance. Even more, imitation's place of supremacy over compliance is seen in the fact that it speaks of Jesus' interest in our personal welfare and growth. If all Jesus required of us was compliance with his commands, we could surmise that his interests lay somewhere but we would not know where. That he requires our imitation of him clearly signals that we are the objects of his interest and affections. We are not the means to some selfish and devious end. Instead, we as a people transformed for the better, are Jesus' desired end brought about by various divine means. There are few illustrations in society and culture that offer a glimpse of the call to follow by imitation. Something that is obvious from these rare cases, parenting for example, is that we naturally cherish and take pride in those things that reflect our image. Of course, this is assuming that what we see is worthy of praise and laud. It is possible that the tendency to cherish our image is grounded in our reflection, though poorly, of God's nature and character. We find that in the created order, God reserves the place of preeminence, for that being he has created in his image. This creature is also the recipient of his deepest affections and fondness. The call to imitation is much more effective than compliance at communicating the value God places on us. Everything in creation by their nature and character reveals something specific about God. Human beings on the other hand have the high honor of presenting a more holistic representation of God. Undoubtedly our descent into rebellion has hindered our capacity to image God fully and completely. Here, we must note the relationship between imitation/image and kinship. Typically, we resemble those we are kin of. Nowhere in scripture do we find any earthly animal or creature, besides humanity, referred to as children of God. To imitate God, is to be his kin. To comply with him is to be his creation. The call to imitate God, is greater than the call to comply because it proclaims divine kinship. We are literally members of God's family.

Another reason imitation is of a higher form than compliance is that it requires we draw close to the object we are called to follow. The closeness is such that it involves the invasion of what one might consider private and personal space. Consider what has occurred in our entrance by the Holy Spirit, through Christ, into the holiest place. The Holy of Holies was the most sacred place in the Jewish temple. The sacrosanct nature of this space was evident in what it housed, the Ark of the covenant, on which sat the Mercy Seat. It was on the Mercy Seat that God's presence rested when he came down to commune with Moses and Israel. The privacy and sanctity of the Holy of Holies is evident in the fact that the High Priest could only enter there once a year. Even then, he had to follow clearly delineated instructions and strict procedures that preserved the holiness of the space and ensured his safety. The sanctity of the Ark and Mercy Seat are substantiated by the account of God's destruction of the Philistines and their gods (1Samuel 5). Another example of the sacredness of God's space is seen in the death of Uzzah. The account of Uzzah's death speaks with great force to the severity of approaching God (2Samuel 6.1-6). Here was a man who lost his life in an act that on a cursory look appears to be most noble. Uzzah lost his life because he held on to the Ark of God's presence to ensure it did not topple over! Pause is necessary to understand and come to terms with God's response to Uzzah. This and other examples reinforce certain matters to be fact. First, approaching God's presence and person is no small matter. Second, a very limited number of people were allowed into the presence of God. Third, those that are invited into God's presence have been accorded an immeasurable honor and sobering responsibility. Fourth, we should ponder the cost, Jesus' death and resurrection, by which we enter his precious presence. Finally, we must understand that one reason God has brought us into his most sacred presence is to imitate him! We are called to pray like him. We are called to give like him. We are called to forgive like him. We are called to show mercy like him. We are called to love and be holy, like him.

Imitation and Discipleship

Reflect on what has occurred in our becoming the very habitation of the spirit of the living God. This is sacred closeness! Intimacy upon intimacy! Without this degree of closeness, the endeavor to copy God in thought, word and deed would be an utter failure. Such closeness can only be understood as fellowship which is a necessary and essential element of imitation. The reality of this close and intense association with God offers us great and beneficial insight. It provides a unique vantage point from which Christian Mentorship (a.k.a. discipleship) may be comprehended and modeled. We will produce healthy Christ disciples when we open and invite people into the deepest recesses of our lives. We must allow our brothers and sisters close enough to see, feel and know our strengths and successes. But even more, we must allow them close enough to observe, analyze and judge our failures and weaknesses. Daunting? Yes, but only through this kind of intimacy and all-access entrance can they learn from us that victory in Christ is not void of failure or weakness, instead it is persevering in faith through failure and weakness. In addition, drawing new believers this close affords them the opportunity to become a better replica of Jesus than we are. They can build on our strengths and avoid our faults. The fact that God grants us all-access into his presence does not make it any less sacred than it was prior to our entrance. Instead through Christ's sacrifice, we are made sacred and forgiven for treating God's presence as common. Also, we are afforded the opportunity to grow in the apprehension of our shared sacredness with God. That is, in Christ we come to realize that God calls us to share in his sacredness and holiness. In discipleship, the shared sacredness between God and his children is reflected in the mutual sacredness of both the mentor and protégé. Therefore, mentors and disciplers need not fear that their protégés will despise them when their faults are discovered, after all those faults take on a holy nature in the light of Christ's death and resurrection. To despise or condemn any Christian for their faults, is to deny the efficacy of Calvary! It is to ignore this fact, in Christ, God sanctified the sins of every true Christian as His to deal with, and deal with them He did. He sanctified sin for a reckoning that was achieved once and for all in Jesus' humiliation, suffering and death. The acceptance of our newfound closeness to God and sacredness of this association is vital to healthy and genuine discipleship. The discipling church consists of mentors who are unafraid of being intimate or being imitated. They give their protégés all-access because they desire the joy of being copied and have no fear of judgment or condemnation. Mentors of this sort are not perfect; they simply have a clear and strong understanding of what it means to possess precious fellowship with God. The discipling church also comprises protégés who know to treat both the virtues and vices of their mentors as sacred elements belonging to the Lord. We find these qualities to be hardly present when it comes to compliance. It is for this reason that our world, though suffering a dearth in followership, will at best reluctantly default to followership by compliance. Compliance divorced of imitation is cold and devoid of deep commitment. Thus, it provides the most ideal conditions for the fomenting of manipulation and hypocrisy. It is no wonder we are leadership drunk and covetous. After all, as a leader I am less likely to be manipulated or hood winked. Forget that in the process I may become the manipulator or hypocrite. Followership of the compliance caliber requires very little from both the leader and follower. Their secret dealings and motives can remain hidden and safe because compliance allows for the maintenance of great distance and detachment. There is relatively little sacrifice of time, treasure and heart, when compliance is compared to imitation.

The closeness required for imitation and replication to be successful, also calls for transparency. Although this transparency is required from both parties, the imitator and the one being imitated, it falls primarily on the latter party to open up. For imitation to be successful, the object being modeled must fully open up their selves. They must lay bare their motives, nature and passions, this is exactly what God accomplishes in sending Jesus Christ to humanity (John 15.15, 17.6, 1Jn 4.8-9). The Christian's knowledge of God immeasurably surpasses that of any people before. God has gone to this extent of making himself known, not for the sole purpose of associating with us and vice versa but also that we may fully imitate him in this life. It is for this reason godliness should not be measured by our natural or spiritual abilities but by how much we resemble our Father. The imitator must then fully commit themselves to two parallel pursuits. First, they must be fully committed to look deeply into what is being revealed (1Jn 1.1-3). Second, they must devote themselves to producing a replica, an imitation, of what they have seen and experienced. Again, we see the primacy of imitation over compliance. It takes courage and selflessness to lay oneself bare to be observed. At the same time, it requires a single-minded focus on the part of the imitator. The imitators must devote themselves to rigorous and exhaustive study of what is being revealed so as to successfully replicate it. In this kind of followership, we see a dynamic back and forth relationship between the follower and the model. The model makes themselves transparent and the imitator exercises diligence in seeking to understand and replicate what is revealed. This effort to understand and replicate communicates worth and value to the model being copied. Neither this dynamic nor its accompanying qualities need be present when followership by compliance is in play. All that is needed is the provision of a set of directives and instructions. You see, imitation followership is symbiotic in nature. It calls for two entities to live together in a relationship that is mutually beneficial. This is not necessarily the case in compliance followership.

Thus far, we have explored the elements and nature of followership. We concluded that followership exists in two primary forms, compliance and imitation. Due to its simplicity and one-dimensional nature, compliance may be understood to be a lower form of followership. We affirmed that followership exists as a higher form in imitation or replication. Imitation followership fosters and displays qualities of intimacy, courage, bravery, transparency and knowledge. These qualities create a relationship that is mutually beneficial and enjoyable for both the imitator and model. We also observed that Jesus called his disciples to both forms of followership. However, we observed that Jesus' call to compliance, carries with it the express purpose of making us into a copy of himself and gifting us with the experience of replicating his life in ourselves and others. Basically, compliance to Christ finds its ultimate purpose in the imitation of Christ. Thus, while affirming the superiority of imitation followership, the New Testament establishes the validity of both forms. In bringing Christian followership under a magnifying glass for a study of its composite parts, it is important to give serious attention to the following caveat, "be careful to refrain from creating a clean separation between compliance and imitation." To sever compliance followership from imitation followership would be to do violence to the teaching of scripture. Furthermore, it would be a misrepresentation of God's call and work in the lives of his family, the church of Christ. The Bible emphatically charges us to obey God's commands. It should be stated again, lest we forget, "it is not possible to imitate Christ without obeying him."

Whether ecclesial or secular, western trends typically spread quickly to other parts of the world. Our present one-sided obsession with leadership is no exception. Already, churches in Asia, the Middle East and Africa are beginning to hold leadership conferences and publish leadership books, while neglecting to develop their members into mature and sober followers. I recently returned from a trip to a country in West Africa. While there I found myself in a recurring conversation with different people concerning the corrupt state of the country. Interestingly enough, the blame for the country's condition was consistently laid at the feet of its leaders. Eventually, I pointed to a few examples of corruption I had seen perpetuated by the average citizenry of the country and asked if the problem was really with the leaders or the people that followed them. Since the people knew their leaders where wrong, why did they copy them? After all, before these officials became leaders, they were everyday citizens. Our God given place of global influence, among his churches, should serve as a motivation to sober up and apply an approach that appreciates both leadership and followership. However, such an approach must still affirm the primacy of followership.

Questions (Imitating Jesus)

1. In what way is the imitation of Christ higher than compliance with Christ?

2. Does the primacy of imitating Christ permit non-compliance with his commands?
   a. Why or Why not?

3. What part do we play in imaging God?

4. What are the possible consequences of discipleship based primarily on compliance?

THE DEARTH OF FOLLOWERSHIP IN THE CHURCH

So, why was I upset at my son for being a follower? And why did a mother feel the need to point out to a four-year-old that she was a leader? Earlier on, I mentioned that our reaction was consistent with western society and its present obsession with leadership. It does not take much to see that our culture is intensely enamored with the idea of leadership. This attitude has given rise to massive investments in, and expenditures of, time, talent, money and energy in the making of leaders. The celebration of leaders does not automatically equate a lack of appreciation for followers. However, it may be the case when followership is not celebrated, taught or emphasized with equal fervor, if at all. This is exactly what we see playing out in present day society and culture. We have an abundance of resources and training materials on leaders and leadership being churned out on a regular basis, all espousing the virtues and indispensability of leadership. There is no lack of conferences offering principles and strategies for developing dynamic and successful leaders. Interestingly, little to nothing of the sort is being done as it concerns followership development. This is true of just about every facet of society and culture. If followership is addressed, it is approached as an aspect of leadership. As a matter of fact, followership is currently studied in certain circles as a field of leadership. In settings such as these, the goal is to equip leaders with tools for influencing people to follow them. Thus, followers are not the intended beneficiary of such sessions or workshops. Ultimately, we are experiencing a serious lack of books, apps or conferences that are specifically geared at inspiring followership and developing followers. Unfortunately, the church is also complicit in this state of affairs. We rarely ever hear any sermons offering biblical principles on followership. We do not hold retreats or conferences that focus on building our character as followers. We have blindly copied society in its negligence to foster a robust culture of followership. Some may suggest the existence of synonymity between discipleship and followership. By this, they posit the argument that the church's ongoing efforts at discipleship reflect her deep commitment to followership. Let's be clear, the fact that disciple means student or follower, does not imply that followership is the same as discipleship. Discipleship may be understood as the process of teaching and enabling others to become like Jesus Christ. This work of teaching and enablement is not only theoretical in nature. It is not simply explaining from scripture matters concerning the life of Jesus to the devout. It also involves, modeling these lessons of Jesus' life in such a way that others are able to emulate. At this point in time, the church's discipleship endeavor is out of balance, due to its obsession with leadership and indifference to followership. This obsession with leadership and indifference to followership has produced a skewered vision of Jesus which we have unwittingly embraced. In this vision, we see every interaction between Jesus and members of his community as an expression and affirmation of his leadership. Therefore, our efforts at developing Christlikeness in one another becomes a mission to develop godly leaders, aka World Changers. We are basically blind to the fact that on a number of occasions Jesus Christ interacted within his culture and society from the position of a follower. Most of the sermons and teachings we hear about Jesus, tend to highlight what we perceive and interpret to be virtues of leadership. Those responsible for discipling supplement these messages with lives that consistently affirm leadership as a quality to be coveted and extolled while downplaying the place of followership in the Christian's life. We fail to see that certain Gospel passages show Jesus as compliant with the mores of his culture and the leaders of his time. For all intents and purposes, we have effectively communicated that followership is not worth celebrating or nurturing. It is not worth the expenditure of our energies and resources to develop. This current state of affairs reveals our utter failure at recognizing leadership and followership as opposite sides of the Christian discipleship coin. One cannot exist without the other. We must seek to be Christ the follower, as much as we seek to be Christ the leader. By celebrating and investing in leadership while ignoring followership, we have unknowingly communicated to one another that followers are at best insignificant and at worst, worthless. And who has ever wanted to be insignificant and worthless? Talk less of having their children live as such. Today, leaders are seen as trendsetters and chart plotters. Followers on the other hand are seen as thoughtless, weak and passive, even baggage. Leaders are held up as role models, followers are not held down, they are simply not recognized at all. Again, this celebratory stance towards leaders and non-verbal derogation of followers is very alive in the church of God. Paul acknowledged the existence of inequality of ability within the church (1Cor 12.20-25) and presented a solution that was to be implemented. The weaker or less significant parts of the church were to be celebrated even more than the prominent parts. By citing Paul's solution, I am not suggesting that followership is of less importance than leadership. As a matter of fact, I will be making the case for its primacy over leadership. I am simply stating that even if a case could be made for order of importance, the lesser should be celebrated even more. Unfortunately, this does not seem to be the current reality in our churches. What we find are adherents and congregations celebrating pastors and teachers of different offices. The church does not seem to be asking how they should celebrate and encourage those that faithfully follow the direction of these leaders. This celebration of Christian leaders may be excused on a national or regional scale. After all, as an institution, it makes sense to some degree that we should have certain people the culture recognizes as the voice and face of the church. However, on a local level, one should expect to see a consistent and genuine celebration of both leadership and followership in the churches. This would reflect an application of Paul's teaching previously mentioned. Sadly, what we witness on a local level is a continued emphasis on celebrating and teaching leadership, while followership as a relevant discipline is neither celebrated nor taught. Given this condition it is no surprise that parents would apply themselves to ensuring their children grow up to be leaders. Am I suggesting that the church stop celebrating its leaders? No. However, we should give serious consideration to what it is we celebrate about are leaders. I think we should celebrate and laud them for faithfully following Jesus and their God-given vision. In doing this, we recognize and affirm that they are great as leaders because they are faithful as followers.

Questions (Dearth of Followership)

1. Do you see evidence of a lack of attention to developing followership in your life?

2. What are some possible benefits of focusing on Jesus' followership qualities?

3. How can a celebration of our leaders foster an appreciation of followership in the church?

DEARTH AND ITS CONSEQUENCES

We've already stated that the continual celebration of leadership is ubiquitous. One apparent effect of this condition is the obvious inability of our society to sustain any movement for the extended period of time needed to bring about lasting change. Historically, movements have proven to be the most necessary and effective drivers of societal change. This is seen to be true whether it be to the benefit or detriment of society and culture. We know that until an idea captures the heart of an overwhelming majority it never becomes reality. Typically, what we find is a mass of people and communities gathering around a particular issue. Eventually this crowd mobilizes into a structured organization, with a leader or cohesive group of leaders set on changing or challenging the status quo. This leader or leadership group have one voice that the organization responds to. However, in today's world we find the opposite occurring. Thanks in large part to technology and social media specifically, we are able to quickly galvanize around an issue. Unfortunately, our covetousness of leadership, has produced too many voices seeking to determine the direction for the mass of people that have gathered. These voices offer differing and often times opposing solutions to the issue in question. Because followership as a skill or discipline is either lacking or underdeveloped within our culture, there is an inability to evaluate and determine the validity of one voice over another. As a result, what occurs next is this great number of people progressively and repeatedly break up into splinter groups incapable of cooperating. Why? No one wants, or knows, how to follow the other. What initially appeared to be a promising movement destined to better society suffers a slow and painful death. It is survived by the dashed hopes of so many. There are two possible reasons for this sorry state of affairs.

First, because followership is neither taught nor celebrated, we lack the skills and capability to discern who the true leaders are, the ones capable of leading us to a better future. Second and most common, is that we lack the virtues necessary to stand down and follow the lead of another. Again, these virtues are lacking because we have failed to emphasize, develop and teach followership as a skill and discipline of great value, one that should be fervently pursued.

Interestingly, there seems to be a dawning awareness that our obsession with leadership is very unhealthy. Coupled with this fledgling awareness is the knowledge of its insidious tendency to put a stop to new movements or societal progress. In what appears to be a sincere attempt to correct this problem, organizations are now being created with loose structures of decentralized leadership, while others are opting to completely forego any attempts at clearly identifying their leaders. In the latter case, the collective determines the goals and directions of these organizations. As is to be expected such groups have been largely ineffective in achieving most of their objectives. This is because leaders like followers are a necessary element to the life of any organization or movement. People decide to follow when clear direction and beautiful vision is laid out before them. Leaders are those responsible for laying out vision and giving direction. To shirk off the mantle of leadership is to effectively ensure the death of any movement, as is to resist the call to follow.

Decentralization of leadership has not fared well either. It lessens the force and voice of such movements. Furthermore, it can result in decision making gridlocks because too many people become involved in the decision-making process. It brings to mind the age-old adage, "too many cooks, spoil the broth." These approaches will neither rid us of our wanton covetousness of leadership nor help in sustaining movements and organizations that serve as the primary drivers for improving the common good.

Up to this point we've addressed our celebration and covetousness of leadership to the detriment of followership. We've seen that this obsession leads to the death of movements, which drive the improvement of society and culture. These movements slowly die out because leaders are needed to guide them to the achievement of a common goal. Are leaders available and ready? Yes. The problem is that there are too many among them who are not true leaders. Strangely, more people in current society identify themselves as leaders than as followers. This situation creates two difficulties that must be ironed out. One of these problems is the arduous task of determining who the true leaders are. In both the Old and New Testaments, we see grave attention is given to the reality of false leaders and the damage they cause. As part of their preparation for entrance and life in the promise land, God gave Israel very specific instructions on how to discern and treat false prophets. Besides kings and priests, the Bible points to the significant role Prophets played as leaders of Israel. They came into prominence when Israel and Judah needed to be called back to godliness and holy living. Also, prophets served to encourage Israel in times of war and even acted as counselors to their kings. One could make the case that of all three leadership roles (king, priest and prophet) prophets played the most prominent part in determining the destiny of the nations of Israel and Judah. The scriptures are filled with an abundance of evidence for the fear and honor Israel, and their kings, gave to the prophets. False prophets consistently caused Israel and Judah to pursue the wrong objectives. At other times the presence and work of false prophets caused God's people to display a high degree of indecision. Surely these factors must have been a major motivation for God's diligence in giving Israel a litmus test for determining true prophets. The destructive consequences suffered by Israel and Judah as a result of the presence and influence of false prophets and insecure kings is similar to what we have today. Due to the coveting and intense clamoring for leadership positions, indecision and the pursuit of false of objectives are very real problems faced by movements, organizations and institutions in our time. Repeated occurrences of these experiences eventually lead to the death of movements. Stagnancy and mirages are extremely effective at breaking the will of a people.

A second problem is that an excess of leaders will result in a failure to amass enough followers to constitute a necessary force for change, a critical mass. In a world where everybody wants to be leader, it is hard to imagine any force strong, large, loud and cohesive enough to bring about a change in the status quo. Instead, we have splinter groups that are insignificant and powerless to achieve anything of lasting benefit. Historically, the majority constituents of any force, military or otherwise, are followers. What we typically see is a few leaders directing and guiding a large number of followers. A movement is composed of the harmonious relationship between the few leaders and the numerous followers working towards the achieving of a common objective. Scripture offers precedent for the concept of an organized movement as composing few leaders and many followers. It shows this to be the healthy and normative constitution of any effective movement and institution. When Moses speaks to God concerning the burden of leading the people of Israel, who numbered at least 600,000, God counsels him to select seventy elders to assist. That's an approximate ratio of one leader or judge for every eight thousand five hundred people! It is hard to imagine that responsibility was not further delegated to leaders responsible for a smaller number of people. Nevertheless, what we see here is a large body of followers with a significantly lesser number of people leading. Our culture and churches have ignored this precedent, opting to produce a movement composing as many leaders as they are followers. In many cases, we have proudly but ignorantly produced institutions and groups consisting more leaders than followers. The end result in such situations? A weak, ineffective and powerless group of people. We must conclude that neither an increase in the numbers of available leaders nor the shirking off of leadership are viable solutions for fixing the problem. None of the approaches formulated by society and culture appear to offer any hope of a repair.

A Misplaced Priority

Questions (Dearth & Its Consequences)

1. Can you think of a time when you experienced or observed the effects produced by an under developed followership ability?

2. Have you ever been in a situation where you felt there were too many leaders?
   a. What was it like?
   b. How was the group able achieve its goal?

3. Have you ever given up a position of leadership because you felt to many people wanted the position?
   a. How did you feel afterwards?
   b. In what ways did your decision benefit the organization or group?
   c. Given the opportunity would you make the same choice?

THE PRIMACY OF FOLLOWERSHIP

Let us consider another approach to reviving the power of movements, one clearly advanced by sacred scripture. This approach involves the recognition and affirmation of the primacy of followership over leadership. Caution must be advised here, in stating that followership has preeminence of place over leadership, I am not suggesting that the Bible calls for a swinging of the pendulum to the opposite and far end. No, scripture does not teach that we should celebrate followership and despise leadership. Instead, we should understand leadership as proceeding from, and jealously guarded by followership. This is to say, followership is the sustaining force, the mother and father, of true and effective leadership. From this position, we can then celebrate the leaders among us, and their indispensable ability to guide and direct. A celebration of this sort gives due deference to the discipline of followership. In this scenario, we would learn to appreciate followership as prerequisite and essential to effective leadership. In other words, we would have created a culture in which followership is recognized as a skillful discipline that must be exercised regularly and masterfully by the successful leaders among us. In this society, neither following nor leading is looked down on. Instead they are celebrated as two elements that harmoniously work together to achieve a common purpose.

In arguing for the Bible's advocacy for the primacy of followership over leadership, the first and most essential point to be stated is that human beings were created to be followers. Genesis agrees with this statement, when its captures the divine conversation, "let us make man in our image, after our likeness" (Gen 1.26-27. ESV). Too often we skip the former part of the divine proclamation and immediately focus on the latter, "let them rule" (Gen 1.26-27. NASB). By this, we unknowingly display our proclivity for grasping at every opportunity to exercise dominion, a word whose meaning we erroneously limit to leadership. However, these scriptures reveal the relationship between our nature and function. We are followers by nature, who have been given the responsibility of exercising dominion. In context, we discover the responsibility of dominion to be our divine enduement to function as stewards. Thus, equating stewardship to leadership without any qualification would be a categorical error. For the simple reason that leadership is one form or expression of stewardship, not the other way around. Therefore, we should not be quick to assume that the exercise of dominion or stewardship is exclusively expressed in the call to lead. All human beings have a divine mandate to steward the earth but not all of us are called to fulfil that mandate through leadership. Many of us show good stewardship through caregiving, others show stewardship by encouraging and nurturing. Some express stewardship when they seek to protect the poor and weak, or nature's beauty and resources. The point here is that stewardship and dominion are not only articulated through leadership.

Nevertheless, the call to leadership is firmly entrenched in humanity's divine call to steward the earth. It is essential for us to understand that the ability to steward properly as leaders is based on the wholesomeness of our nature as followers. Unfortunately, we have failed to maintain this distinction between nature and function. As a result, we have given up who we are to be, for what we are to do. But it is impossible to do what one must, without knowing and having a firm handle on who one is. As a matter of fact, we do because we are! Since leadership is a function of followership, it is essential that we give the utmost attention and effort to ensuring the wholeness and maturation of our follower-nature. If this nature is broken or wanting in any sense, our ability to lead effectively is greatly hampered. In other words, correct and effective leadership is built on the foundation of followership. If the foundation is faulty, the house and all its contents will eventually crumble.

Why is leadership the only expression of stewardship that seems to attract such inordinate attention and affection? Leaders are typically first in line and therefore appear to set the course or direction of a movement. I believe, it is this desire to set the course, to be masters of our destiny and that of others, that compels us to an intense covetousness of leadership. This desire to be mastered by none and master of all, lays the groundwork for a displacement of followership. We ignore the fact that man and woman are made to image the godhead. That is to say, we exist first and foremost as an imitation, a copy, of God. Our effective exercise of dominion and leadership in the world is contingent on our faithfulness to copy God, that is, to follow Him. This is because in exercising leadership, we are simply revealing one aspect of God's character. Thus, doing it well requires that we follow him well. If successful leadership is based on following God, it stands to reason that a necessary prerequisite of effective leadership is the experience of the revelation of God. It is quite obvious that one cannot imitate, what they have not or cannot see. To follow God, one must first see him and then follow. Remember that even though God intended for man, created with a following nature, to exercise ruler-ship, He still needed to reveal to Adam what this entailed. Thus, we see Adam tending the garden and naming the animals at God's behest. The Revelation of God and the imperative to follow are constant themes in scripture as it concerns the call to steward, in its various expressions. The reception or confirmation of the Abrahamic covenant experienced by the Patriarchs, Abraham, Isaac and Jacob are all preceded by some sort of an encounter with God that can only be described as revelatory in nature. In each case, they must choose whether to believe and follow God's command or not. The establishment of these men as Patriarchs and by extension leaders of the people of faith is founded upon two credentials, their revelation encounters with God and their choice to faithfully follow in obedience. We see this same pattern play out in the cases of Moses and Joshua. Prior to becoming leaders of their people and great men of renown, they each experience the revelation of God and answer the call to follow in obedience. Their greatness was cemented in history and for all time by their faithful following of God. These encounters clearly prove that genuine, effective and successful leadership is based on faithful ongoing followership. In other words, followership has pride of place over leadership, at every time, in every place and in every culture! It is important to note that the nature of followership referenced here includes both compliance and imitation. We will always find that leadership is consistently lost or made ineffective, when those to whom it is given, attempt its exercise independent of followership. The ineptitude and loss of leadership in the absence of followership is a principle as old as creation.

Leadership is "Followery" by Nature

It is possible that our current celebration and focus on leadership is simply an outworking of our most ancient sin, autonomy, the desire to discover and define life independent of God. This is obviously a perversion, since leadership is heteronomous in nature. In referring to leadership as heteronomous, I mean that it is sustained by adhering and depending on God. Leadership is built, guided and sustained by followership, to make it autonomous is to effectively nullify it. Just as failure, pain and destruction followed our progenitors in their bid for autonomous leadership, we find ourselves experiencing a similar fate when we model their error. Leadership that fosters life and productivity will always be found established on followership, specifically of the kind that complies with God's commands and imitates His character, as well as his nature.

Basically, before anyone can be a leader, they must be a follower. It is important to understand that this principle does not have a termination point. That is to say, the day a leader stops following, marks the day he or she begins to lose their place of effective influence and successful leadership. We see both these principles clearly play out in the lives of Adam and Eve. We've already addressed the fact that their leadership and dominion was firmly established on their nature as God's image bearers. Imaging God obviously required that they experienced intimacy with God and learned of him based on what he disclosed to them. Scripture reveals this to have been the state of things originally. The Bible reveals that God walked in the garden in which he had placed humanity (Genesis 3.8-9). We can surmise from the account in Genesis that God was in the garden to fellowship with humanity. Notice that God calls out for Adam, "Where are you?" Furthermore, we see that Adam and Eve hide when they heard God walking in the garden. It is as if they expected that he would come looking for them. Additionally, we know that God was man's sole source of knowledge and information. This is evident in God's response (Genesis 3.10-11), when Adam states his reason for hiding, "Who told you... have you eaten from the tree?" The scriptural evidence in Genesis clearly lends credence to the belief that God was present in the garden to fellowship with Adam and Eve.

The consequence of humanity's quest for self-determination was not only the loss of the position of leadership over God's creation. In addition to being stripped of authority, Adam and Eve also lost the ability to function as leaders and stewards. All of this was due to humanity's quest for self-determination and autonomy. This quest is clearly captured in the exchange between the Serpent and Eve.

"The serpent was the shrewdest of all the wild animals the LORD God had made. One day he asked the woman, "Did God really say you must not eat the fruit from any of the trees in the garden?" "Of course, we may eat fruit from the trees in the garden," the woman replied. "It's only the fruit from the tree in the middle of the garden that we are not allowed to eat. God said, 'You must not eat it or even touch it; if you do, you will die.'" "You won't die!" the serpent replied to the woman. "God knows that your eyes will be opened as soon as you eat it, and you will be like God, knowing both good and evil." The woman was convinced. She saw that the tree was beautiful, and its fruit looked delicious, and she wanted the wisdom it would give her. So, she took some of the fruit and ate it. Then she gave some to her husband, who was with her, and he ate it, too. At that moment their eyes were opened, and they suddenly felt shame at their nakedness. So, they sewed fig leaves together to cover themselves." (Genesis 3.1-7 New Living Translation)

The Serpent shrewdly brings into question God's motive for keeping Adam and Eve away from the tree of the knowledge of Good and Evil. Furthermore, he proclaims the virtues of the tree as giving Godlike wisdom. Eve responds to these claims by reaching for the fruit, indicating her distrust of Yahweh's character. She would rather have her life in her hands, than trust it to the character and hands of God. In this action she reveals humanity's intense and violent drive to be masters of their destiny. The desire to live and lead free of any constraint or guiding influence. It is here we see a coup to move leadership from a foundation of followership (Heteronomy) to a foundation of self-determination (Autonomy). An ill-conceived notion to transform the very nature of leadership from heteronomy divine, to mortal autonomy. Alas, the accidental invention of spiritual alchemy! You see leadership and followership are two parts of the same structure. In attempting to move leadership from its natural foundation, Adam and Eve unwittingly destroyed the whole structure.

By endeavoring to change the very nature of leadership, Adam and Eve created a completely new reality, subjugation and slavery founded on fear and shame! This becomes clear as the biblical narrative progresses.

A Misplaced Priority

"So, she took some of the fruit and ate it. Then she gave some to her husband, who was with her, and he ate it, too. At that moment their eyes were opened, and they suddenly felt shame at their nakedness. So, they sewed fig leaves together to cover themselves. When the cool evening breezes were blowing, the man and his wife heard the LORD God walking about in the garden. So, they hid from the LORD God among the trees. Then the LORD God called to the man, "Where are you?" He replied, "I heard you walking in the garden, so I hid. I was afraid because I was naked." (Genesis 3.6b-10 New Living Translation)

Upon consuming the fruit from the tree of knowledge of good and evil, one would expect to see human beings stewarding and leading on their own initiative. Instead we find our ancestors frantically working at covering their shame. Interestingly, our grasping for, and eventual acquisition of divine ability, the capacity to discern good and evil, resulted in our loss of ability to steward ourselves talk less of the creation. Our attempt to lead autonomously resulted in a complete change of orientation.

God created us as followers charged with stewardship of the earth, but we inadvertently transformed ourselves into slaves driven by shame and fear to self-destruction. In a bid to guide our continued leadership and stewardship of the creation, God comes down to reveal himself and fellowship with humanity. But what do we find? Our parents are no longer interested in leadership or stewardship of the creation, at least not on God's terms. No, they are now mastered by fear and shame. Their new masters set them to the task of building and maintaining secrecy. The abandonment of their original charge for a grievous one is seen in their acts of concealment. We see it in the veiling of their perceived vulnerability and the concealment of their very selves from God. Leadership is anything but concealment or secrecy. Leadership by nature is open and public, it demands attention. The quest to be a leader without being a follower is doomed to failure, it is simply not possible. Autonomous leadership is a myth. Unfortunately, society at large and countless Christians, are either oblivious to this timeless truth or, even worse, have stubbornly chosen to ignore it.

Satan by use of fear and shame is able to take the seat of dominion once held by humanity. We find that the creation is now under the sway of sin and ultimately the devil. Scripture lends support to this notion of Satan's rule over the current system of the world (John 12.31, 2Corinthians 4.4, Ephesians 2.2, 1John 5.19). By seeking to lead without following God, Adam and Eve end up relinquishing their dominion to Satan. He in turn, sets up a wicked cosmic system that enslaves humanity and stands in rebellion against God. Satan's purpose is the destruction of humanity and the beautiful world God created (John10.10). Evidence of Satan's dominion over the current order of things is seen in the perpetuation of our continuous attempt at autonomous leadership. Did you noticed that in Genesis, Adam and Eve attempt to cover their nakedness with leaves (Genesis 3:7; 3:22)? The inadequacy of this effort is evident in the fact that God clothes them with a covering of his making. This attempt at covering a perceived vulnerability is still being played out today among people, Christians included, dedicated to autonomous leadership. Instead of looking to God to help their real and perceived weaknesses, they look to themselves. A startling example of this pursuit for autonomy-based leadership is seen in the life of Jeroboam (1Kings 11-12; 13.33-34). In response to Solomon's repeated acts of idolatry, God determined to give kingship of a large portion of the then United Israel to someone else. Ten out of eleven tribes are to be given to Jeroboam, an industrious man who served as one of Solomon's officials. God assures Jeroboam that he will be a successful and effective leader whose ruler-ship will continue beyond his lifetime. All Jeroboam has to do is listen to God, follow his directions and obey his commands. For Jeroboam's leadership to succeed, it must be heteronomous in nature, it must be followership based. To be a lasting and effective leader, Jeroboam must be a lasting and effective follower. His leadership is a function of his nature as a follower! The story of Jeroboam could have ended here, happily ever after, simply by following God. Unfortunately, this is not the case. Jeroboam perceives a strategic weakness in his position. God gave him dominion of eleven tribes but left Judah to be ruled by David's descendants. As it stands,

A Misplaced Priority

Jerusalem is the spiritual capital of the Jewish people and it is located in Judah. God had sanctioned Jerusalem as Israel's place of religious pilgrimage. It was here, the Jewish people were to observe the festivals God had instituted, as well as participate in temple worship. Jeroboam feared that when the people of the ten tribes, subjects of his kingdom, went to Jerusalem to fulfil their religious duties, the king of Judah would turn them against him. The end of this would be the loss of his throne and ultimately his life. It does not take much to see that Jeroboam was a master of strategy and an expert in the use propaganda. However, his fears were completely unfounded, especially in light of the fact that his reign was established on neither strategy nor propaganda. Jeroboam's kingdom was built on the Word of God and it was on this same word that it would be sustained. What was the word of God? Follow me faithfully! But Jeroboam sought to sustain his dominion using means recommended by his counselors. He carried out a devious plan, prevent his subjects from going to Jerusalem by offering them false gods, false temples and a false priesthood. In a bid to sustain his hold on power Jeroboam created a new and false religion for Israel! By doing this, Jeroboam set about to establish autonomous leadership. The utter failure of his leadership and destruction of his dynasty (1Kings 13.33-34) must serve as a warning against the impulse to covet leadership while denigrating followership, its source and custodian. One might think to say that Jeroboam's sin was idolatry, not a bid for autonomous leadership. Such a response fails to recognize that autonomous leadership is a most insidious form of idolatry. It is an attempt to make one's self into God. Remember, this was the seductive nature of the first attempt at autonomous leadership, "and you will be like God..." (Genesis 3.5b).

Another instance that captures the myth and impossibility of autonomous leadership or leadership by self-determination, is found in the life of Moses. At the age of forty, Moses a child born to Israeli slaves is a prince of Egypt. Compelled by an uncanny awareness of a divine call to liberate Israel from captivity (Acts 7.20-25), he murders an Egyptian. Following this incident, he assumes to act as a mediator and judge between two disputing Israelis. He set about this work of deliverance without having experienced God's revelation of Himself. Thus, Moses starts out as a leader incapable of following God because he does not know him. Moses' unfamiliarity with God is captured in their initial conversation which occurs later on (Exodus 3.2-15). In addition, all Moses has to go on is an inkling of a call. He really had no way of knowing with the minutest bit of certainty that God had called him. But for the grace of God, this attempt at autonomous leadership could have ended up in his literal destruction. The very people he had sought to save rejected him (Exodus 2.14) and those he had rejected sought to kill him. He absconds from Egypt while simultaneously abandoning his ambitious but foolhardy quest at autonomous leadership. Further along, we will see that this experience left Moses with a deep aversion to leadership as a whole, even that of a heteronomous nature. Moses' failed venture into leadership later caused him to doubt that the all-powerful God could possibly make a success of him. Such is the destructive character of autonomous leadership. It has the very real potential to cause us to despise our most noble destiny and call from God.

Moses' flight from Egypt was precipitated by a question posed to him by a fellow Israeli, "who made you a ruler and judge over us?" This question may be rephrased to say, "Who do you follow, that we should follow you?" The justification for this paraphrase becomes evident forty years later in Moses' life. At this point he is an eighty-old sheepherder who has quite the encounter with God. The details of this meeting reveal a lot concerning the dynamic relationship between followership and leadership. God reveals Himself to Moses and states the purpose for his visit. He has come down to liberate Israel from their Egyptian captors and to give them a place they will call home. Imagine! What Moses had initially sought to accomplish in his own power, was a task that necessitated God's descending from heaven. This fact reveals the height of arrogance and the utter foolishness of questing after autonomous leadership. Moses had attempted to accomplish a task only God could. He sought to liberate and lead a people only God could! God reveals that his intention is to use Moses as the instrument of his act of liberation, thus, the Mosaic call, "Come now therefore" (Exodus 3.10). This introduction serves as an indicator of Moses' call to a follower-based leadership quest. He must follow God to function effectively in dominion over Egypt and stewardship of Israel. Moses expresses his reluctance and points to his various weaknesses as reasons for why God should send someone else. Incredible! This is the same fellow who forty years earlier had zealously sort to accomplish the same feat. Moses' unwillingness reflects the extent to which his initial experience negatively impacted his self-image and sense of compassion. Who am I? Who are you? What if they question my credibility? What of my inabilities? The preceding questions cover the range of Moses' excuses and echo the rejection he suffered at the hands of his brothers forty years earlier. Granted, God firmly and reassuringly rebuts each of Moses' reasons or fears. However, Moses' doubts reflect the extent of emotional, mental and spiritual damage one will suffer when they pursue autonomous leadership. In Moses, we find a man trained to live as a prince of the greatest nation on earth at the time, content to live as a sheepherder, an outlier. Contentment is a virtue when it is compelled by a humble spirit. Moses was living a false contentment because its motivation was humiliation and fear. Moses suffered from a broken and ruined spirit. Here was a man of great power, in word and deed (Acts 7.22b NASB), reduced to sheepherding because he presumed to lead autonomously. Due to God's grace and kind patience Moses is able to repent of his paralyzing fear. Moses' repentance is not simply a change of mind and attitude, it stands as an act of God's gracious healing of a man who was irreparably damaged. May God in his mercy do the same for those of us who have been seduced by the lure and false glory of autonomous leadership. So, Moses gradually yields to God's urging and goes on this mission with him. Not only does Israel accept and follow Moses this time, they also gained their freedom. Follower based, or heteronomous leadership renders personal weakness meaningless (1Corinthians 12.9-10). For the simple reason that one's effectiveness does not depend on their capacity; on the contrary, it depends on the capacity of the one they follow. Similar to Moses, we must be cognizant of who we follow. Like Israel, we must ensure that before we follow anyone, regardless of their accomplishments and power, we know who they follow. This is the first and most important principle of godly followership. Israel could have followed Moses because he was a man of great power; they could have followed him because he was a man of great learning; they could have followed because he would kill for them; they could have followed him because he would keep the peace. But they did not, if they had, they would have ended up with a man who would desert them at the first sign his life was in danger. One who would not hesitate to quickly flee at the first sign of resistance. Despite Moses' great achievements and power, he was a man deeply attuned to his vulnerability. Like Adam and Eve, and like all of us, compelled by fear, he would go to great lengths to ensure his safety from a perceived threat. This is simply the intended end of autonomous leadership, our destruction! An end that we, unlike our first parents, are now aware off and can avoid. Like a moth to a flame, our culture is being lured to the false promise of autonomous leadership. Surprisingly, countless

Christians are following this wicked and rebellious trend.

In juxtaposing the escapades of forty-year-old Moses (Moses, the younger) against that of eighty-year-old Moses (Moses, the elder), the first thing that stands out is the specificity and clarity of mission possessed by the latter. Moses, the younger, has a simple but strong sense or awareness that he is supposed to liberate Israel. He has no clue how to go about doing this or where he would be taking them. Moses, the elder, receives clear and precise direction, articulated step by step, on where he will be leading Israel and how he will be leading them. In other words, he possesses what we would refer to as clearly defined mission and vision statements. Moses' God given vision statement is for Israel to be a people transformed from captives to worshippers. His God given mission statement is to follow God's directives for liberating Israel from Egypt and bring them to a place where they will worship God.

Additionally, we notice that Moses the younger's, attempt at liberating Israel was based on self-determination. Somehow, he knew God wanted to use him in liberating Israel, so he determined to accomplish this goal dependent on his own ability. On the other hand, Moses, the elder, cares nothing about returning to Egypt for the deliverance of Israel but has to be prompted and strongly urged. Here Moses, exercises followership by complying with God's command. This contrast points at autonomous leadership as indicative of spiritual immaturity and/or insensitivity. In speaking of those qualified to serve as elders (leaders), Paul warns Titus not to select any converts that are new to the faith as a means of ensuring they are protected from the temptation of pride (1Ti 3.6 NASB). Keep in mind that the comparison and contrast of Moses, the younger against the elder, is not to highlight their age difference. Instead, it spotlights their difference in maturity emphasized by the contrast in their experiences of God and His people. Moses, the younger is quick to run headlong into a ministry endeavor. Guided by his past experiences, Moses the elder is more cautious about jumping into an endeavor, regardless of how exciting. He takes the time and effort to consider his abilities and shortcomings. Furthermore, he is diligent to ensure that he is being called by God and not his adventurous impulse. In present church culture, many Christians erroneously identify this impulse to adventure as a prompting from the Holy Spirit for them to act. That we would all learn to walk like Moses the elder, reining our enthusiasm with the exercise of discernment, a sober awareness of our limitations and honest prayers.

Finally, there is a stark contrast in Moses' answer to the question "who do you follow, that we should follow you?" Moses, the younger, responds to this question by fleeing, due in large part to the fact that he does not have an answer. In contrast, Moses, the elder, stands unshaken, answering squarely with undeniable and awe-inspiring credentials. The lesson here is that autonomous leadership is unable to bear under the inquiry for credibility and authentication. In autonomous leadership the responsibility for authentication falls on the individual who claims to be a leader. They must supply clear and sufficient evidence showing that they are fully capable of accomplishing the task at hand. Follower based leadership places the onus of credibility and authentication on God. When we lead by following, the one we follow provides our authentication and establishes our authority. The manner of God's calling in this matter is inconsequential. That is to say, whether God's call is flagrantly overt or unsettlingly covert, he consistently proves the veracity and authority of those he calls.

Legacy's Alienation from Followership

An aspect of Christ's salvific work is the restoration of humanity to a place of intimacy with God and exercise of dominion over the created order. Thus, it is in following Jesus Christ that humankind regains its function as leader and steward of God's world. In Christ, we see that God is faithful to establish and confirm the church's role as salt and light to the world. Time after time, we see a trail of evidence that testifies to the church's role in guiding and pointing society down the right path. Whether it be in assisting with the abolition of slavery, the part she played in the civil rights movement or her current endeavors in social justice issues. In following Christ, we recognize that an agenda has already been established. It is not about us glorifying or satisfying ourselves. Instead we are to show the magnificence and goodness of God to a dying world. Recognition of the call to follow this divine agenda should work as a buffer against the temptation to build a legacy for one's self while leading God's people. In many Christian circles, people speak of leaving behind some kind of a legacy. The question repeatedly asked is, "How do you want to be remembered?" Truth be told, we have no need to concern ourselves with leaving behind a legacy by which we might be remembered. As followers, our job is to ensure that we pass on the legacy Christ left us. Hence, if anything must be remembered, let it be the preeminence of our faithful God and savior, Jesus Christ, and the mandate to diligently follow him. It is only in following him that we truly become a city on a hill offering guidance and deliverance to a generation bound by vice and death. I recently had the opportunity to sit and talk with Lloyd Ziegler, the founder of Masters Commission International Network. This Network consist of several Discipleship and ministry preparatory schools all over the world. I graduated from one of those schools, over a decade ago, and it is difficult to place a value on what I learned while in the program. So, you can imagine my excitement at having a sit down with a man of such stature. When we met that day, I was immediately aware of how unassuming and welcoming he was. During our conversation, he said something that struck me, "I want to die empty and I want to be forgotten. I want God to know my name." Here is a man that is loved and respected by countless people all over the world. God is using him to inspire generations, to know Jesus and make Jesus known. These generations of Christ followers are his offering to the Lord. His desire is not to be commemorated by men but to be celebrated by God. May this be true for us all.

Questions (The Primacy of Followership)

1. In what specific ways do you think recognizing you're a follower can improve your leadership?

2. How does revelation or vision enable followership and leadership?

3. What are some everyday tell-tale signs of autonomous (self-determined) leadership?

4. Compare and contrast the leadership/followership experiences of the younger and elder you.

FOLLOWING ONE ANOTHER

Thus far into our exploration, we have chiefly focused on followership in relationship to God. Most Christians have no problem affirming as fact that effective and sustained leadership depends on whether or not God is followed. The problem arises in our failure to see the correlation between our followership of God and followership of neighbors. By followership of neighbors, I am referring to following those brothers and sisters among us who have been called and gifted with the ability to lead. For many of us, our faithfulness to follow God does not translate to our following of other people. While we strive to comply with God's commands and imitate his character, we have little to no desire for compliance with the directions of fellow human beings. We would rather have others comply with us than vice versa. Herein lies the rub, the truthfulness of our desire to follow God is affirmed by our followership of our neighbors. In other words, we cannot possibly follow the God we cannot see, if we are unable or unwilling to follow our neighbors that we can see. The previous statement should have a familiar ring; it is a twist on 1 John 4.20. In this passage, the Apostle makes an impressive declaration. He affirms the impossibility of loving the invisible God without first and primarily loving our visible neighbors. This statement is neither local nor subjective; rather it is in an objective and governing principle that nurtures our ability to comprehend and apprehend spiritual realities. It is saying that to possess a healthy understanding and interaction with spiritual realities, we must first correctly understand and interact with the natural and visible world. The certainty of this principle is affirmed when John refers to those who claim to love God but hate their neighbors as liars. Nicodemus' secret encounter with Jesus, further validates this principle. Jesus, teacher par excellence, presents a question that affirms this truth as a principle, "If I told you earthly things and you do not believe, how will you believe if I tell you heavenly things?" (John 3.12 NASB). Paul applies this same principle of spiritual apprehension through natural interaction while laying out the case for the wrath and judgment of God on the rebellious. He teaches that the visible and tangible creation makes apparent the invisible attributes of God (Romans 1.18-24). This passage shows that failure to understand and appreciate the tangible inevitably leads to an incapacity to apprehend the divine.

The idea that proper interaction and comprehension of the tangible serves to enhance interaction with the divine holds true for followership as much as it does for love or belief. The fact that we are made in the image of God, who is a community consisting of three persons-- Father, Son and Holy Spirit-- offers a first glimpse into our need for comprehending the intangible through the tangible. In the trinity, we see the Son willfully following the Father (John 5.19 NASB), and the Holy Spirit willfully following the Son (John 16.12-15 NASB). It is important to keep in the forefront of our minds that this act of following does not necessarily equate superiority or hierarchy. As a matter of fact, Jesus speaks of the glory he shared with the Father prior to his incarnation (John 17.5 NASB). Paul also addresses Christ's willful subjection of himself to the Father and his purposes (Philippians 2.5-11 NASB). Our ability to submit to those with apparent leadership ability is the expression of the followership-leadership dynamic that exist within the Trinity. Essential to this dynamic is the absence of hierarchy and the strong presence of willful and voluntary engagement from both parties. As Christians, we are mandated to model our lives after Christ's (1John 2.6). In him, we see a relinquishing of leadership, power and authority, not only to serve but also to follow. Paul holds up this followership-leadership relationship between the Father and Jesus as a model for us to live out in our relationships with one another (Philippians 2.5-11 NASB).

The incarnation of Christ, the act in which the Word becomes flesh and dwells with humanity (John 1.14 NASB) proves to be extremely helpful in capturing the truthfulness of comprehending the intangible through the tangible. Scripture declares that Christ Jesus came in the flesh to pay the price for our sins. This is a fundamental truth that must be accepted by anyone who claims to be a Christian. As a matter of fact, John the Apostle when tackling the heresy of Gnosticism, sets forth as a litmus test for the authenticating of prophets and teachers their confession that Christ lived bodily. In his first letter to the Corinthians (1 Corinthians 15), Paul squarely rest the reality of our salvation on the bodily life, death and resurrection of Jesus. For the most part, we have remained faithful in highlighting and affirming this truth. This is especially evident in our evangelistic and gospel proclamation. In sharing the good news of Jesus Christ, we have been careful to communicate as historical fact that He lived, died and resurrected bodily. All of these establish as fact that only through faith in Christ has God purposed for spiritual power and realities to be experienced. And these experiences occur in our holy interactions with natural and tangible realities.

Furthermore, the Bible presents another reason and benefit of Jesus' incarnation to be the knowledge of God. Through Jesus we gain intimate and experiential knowledge of God. When Philip ask Jesus to show him and the other disciples the Father, Jesus points to himself, "He who has seen me has seen the Father..." (John 14.8-9). Here Jesus is teaching that to have him in their presence is to have God in their presence. To have seen and fellowshipped with him was to see and fellowship with God, the Father. He completely reveals all of God in human form. This is glorious truth. We can know with certainty how God feels and will react to a matter by seeking to understand how Christ felt and reacted to the same or something similar. What is God's response to sin? Based on Christ's response to sin, we can surmise that "seventy times seven times" God will mercifully forgive and simultaneously call us, the penitent, to sin no more (Matthew 18.21-35, John 8.10-11). Our apprehension of this facet of God's posture toward humanity is only possibly through our interaction with the incarnate Christ. Here we see our ability to interact with the invisible God is made possible only through our comprehension of Jesus the Christ, who once was both visible and tangible. We can follow the intangible, only by following the tangible. We see then that the Word not only "became flesh and dwelt among us" (John 1.14a). He also became flesh to dwell *with* us and vice versa. By following those among us that are called to lead, we prove our ability and willingness to follow God. Thus, we lie to ourselves when we say we follow God, who we cannot see, when we fail to follow those brothers and sisters among us that he has enabled to lead.

Another reason we should work to follow those among us that God has called and gifted to be leaders is simply that he commands it. Our sovereign, all powerful creator and loving father commands. Our appropriate and wise response should always be joyful obedience. Sometimes, we are tempted to be believe that an understanding of God's reasons for acting or requiring something of us should serve as a prerequisite for obedience. Such an attitude allows for pride to greatly hinder our communion with God. It places stipulations and limits on our loyalty to the one who freely gave himself for our sakes. This posture also neglects to consider God's place as supreme ruler of creation. We are his to do with as he wills. God would be completely justified and righteous if he decided to keep hidden his purposes.

Furthermore, we would do well to remember that God's commands always serve to benefit those who believe and trust in him. In light of our current allergic reaction to followership, this truth should offer great comfort as we seek to obey God's commands.

Questions (Following One Another)

1. Do you believe hierarchy to be a necessary element in the leader-follower dynamic? Explain why?

2. Do you find following God to be easier than following another human being? Explain why?

3. In what ways could following human leaders aid in following God?

PRINCIPLES OF GODLY FOLLOWERSHIP

Assuming that a clear understanding of the nature and imperative of followership has been set down, we will now explore its character and nature. Followership is typically believed to constitute little more than doing what one is told or copying what one is presented; however, this rudimentary perception of followership rest squarely on a failure to recognize it as a discipline, skill and virtue. This failure stands in stark contrast to leadership which countless ministries and a whole industry have held up as an essential discipline for both church and secular success.

At the core, a follower is someone who complies with-- and/or imitates-- others. However, there is such a thing as godly and wise followership. Followership of this sort ensures that we safely arrive at the appointed and desired goals outlined by God or that are in harmony with his nature. The Bible contains several examples of godly followership. These examples show godly followership to be active and dynamic, culminating in deeper communion with the Father, divine favor, prosperity and the flourishing of society. One instance of this kind of followership is found in the relationship between Elijah and Elisha (1Kings 19.19-21, 2Kings 2). Elisha's faithfulness to follow Elijah did not simply result in his personal success, the nations of Israel and Judah benefitted immensely from it (2Kings 3). Besides these nations, we see a number of individuals benefitting from Elisha's faithful following of Elijah (2Kings 4, 2Kings 5.1-19). Scripture also contains examples of bad or passive followership. Followership of this sort typically leads to estrangement from God, pronouncements of judgement and the eventual destruction of society. Godly followership is dynamic, wise and disciplined. It ensures that the right person is guiding us to the right goals. It possesses a number of traits that work in synergy to bring about a beautiful end. The traits and characteristics of godly followership presented here are by no means exhaustive. Nevertheless, they are found to be consistently present in the biblical narratives depicting cases in which followership led to a successfully and noble end. Their permanence brings us to an obvious conclusion, the success of our quests rest heavily on ensuring that we apply these traits, before following and while following anyone that seeks or holds a position of leadership.

Self and Situational Awareness

Wise and godly followers possess self and situational awareness. Basically, they possess a deep appreciation of their strengths and weaknesses. They know what they are able to do and have no qualms owning up to what is beyond their ability. In a sense you can say they possess humility. This trait is essential to good followership because it serves to keep in check the wicked tendency to grasp for positions of influence, power and preeminence. One way self-awareness is expressed in the church is in our recognition of individual spiritual gifts. This awareness not only compels us to use our ability to serve others, it also gives us permission to passionately welcome help from others. Self-awareness enables us to understand what we have and what we need. My willingness to follow is ignited when I realize what I desperately need and am convinced that someone can help me acquire that goal.

The pricelessness of self-awareness is especially evident in the case of the Pharisees' responses to Jesus. Their lack of self-awareness was evident in their repeated failure to recognize themselves as sinners (Matthew 9.13, John 9.39-41). This blindness made the message of their need for a savior ridiculous. In their eyes they were righteous. The thought that they needed to be liberated from the dominion of sin was utter rubbish. Their apparent failure to recognize they were slaves of sin and unrighteousness led to their unwillingness to trust and follow Jesus. Imagine the devastating loss. It is through self-awareness that the follower recognizes the need to bring about a change in their status. By it they gain not only a consciousness of who they are, but also, who they are not. Self-awareness may not always compel us to follow but it will serve as a driving force compelling us to pursue the change we need. A lot of times that change involves our moving from one place to another. Such moves our not always physical; they can take an abstract form. For example, the need to change thought patterns, habits and attitudes. Most times, we need someone, a leader, to guide us safely and successfully through these transitions.

While self-awareness chiefly concerns our personal being, situational awareness focuses more on our surroundings and environment. A person may possess strong character, interpersonal skills and talent, yet the conditions they live in may be unfavorable to their overall health. These external conditions may hamper their ability to experience life at its fullest. We have countless inspiring stories of people who possessed a certain talent but were living in deplorable conditions. Unable to harness these talents, they were of no benefit to themselves or society. Their state of affairs remained the same until their surroundings changed or they were moved to a more conducive environment. I believe this is one reason so many people flee their countries of birth and move to the United States. A great portion of these people have contributed in immeasurable ways to the prosperity of this country. Their contributions speak to the abundance of character and talents they possessed prior to their arrival in the States. Yet, it took a change in their situation for these great assets to be nurtured and eventually flourish to the benefit of all.

Situational-awareness opens the follower's eyes to the state of their affairs, the condition in which they exist. If these conditions are conducive, there is little motivation or need to be led. If the opposite, the willingness to be led is extremely high. As a matter of fact, an awareness of an unfavorable or difficult situation will drive us to cry out for relief. This fact is played out in Israel's enslavement by Egypt (Exodus 2.23). The pain of abuse and suppression suffered by Israel resulted in their crying out to God. In contrast, a lack of situational awareness can lead to blissful ignorance and eventual destruction. The seventh chapter of Joshua records an interesting encounter that captures the importance of situational-awareness. Joshua had just led Israel in a successful military campaign against what until that time had been considered an impregnable city, Jericho. Their next stop was a relatively small town called Ai (Joshua 7.2-3). Israel was soundly trounced by the people of this town! Why? It wasn't a lack of proper military strategy or planning. Israel was unaware that their situation or circumstances had changed. It was in communion with God that Joshua discovered this change. Israel lost to Ai because they were now under a divine curse (Joshua 7.12). Prior to this battle Israel had God's favor and pleasure but the disobedience of one of their citizens caused God to turn against them. Unaware of this change in their circumstances, Israel went to war against the enemy. These examples serve to drive home the importance of situational-awareness and their relationship to good followership. Do we have a clear understanding of our current circumstances? Are we satisfied or dissatisfied? Are we crying out to God for a deliverer? Or are we like Israel, going into battle under the assumption that all is well? Another instance in scripture that proves to be very sobering as it concerns situational awareness is the state of the Sadducees. This influential Jewish faction did not believe in the resurrection or spirit beings! (Acts 23.8) Sadly, there are currently many like this in our culture. The devil and his hordes are wreaking havoc in their families, places of work and churches. And they are completely ignorant of the fact that there is a real enemy feverishly working to steal, kill and destroy all they hold precious. We need not look for a demon in every circumstance and issue we face. However, it is important that we recognize the existence of wicked spiritual forces and their goal (2Corinthians 2.11, 2Corinthians 11.14, 1Peter 5.8).

Self-awareness and situational-awareness give us a clear picture of the condition of our person and circumstances. From this picture we can better determine, if we need to be led, where we need to be led and by whom we must be led.

A Misplaced Priority

Vision

Vision is another trait at work in godly followership. It is a clear mental image of the future or what the future could be. It might seem strange to consider vision a trait the follower should possess. One might even argue that the follower's possession of vision negates the need for a leader. At this juncture, it would be helpful to note that vision and execution are two distinct abilities. A follower may possess one or the other, a leader must harness both. In speaking of vision as a trait of followership, it may be helpful to consider it as existing in two forms, General and Specific.

General Vision refers to one's possession of a vague or general desired outcome. Specific Vision, on the other hand, refers to the possession of a specific desired outcome. A person who desires to attend college or acquire employment has General Vision. In contrast, someone with Specific Vision desires to attend a certain college or acquire a particular position within a specific company. Good followership requires that one possess General Vision at the very least. As a matter fact General Vision is a prerequisite to following correctly. The follower must possess a general idea of what it is they want. Their desired end must not be dictated to them, as this may lead to their being manipulated. Besides the possibility of being manipulated, having one's desires and future goals determined by another will make them completely dependent, lacking any sense of self-reliance and worth. Furthermore, knowing and determining what you want for your life, speaks to the fact that you are responsible for it. To let someone else determine your desire and purpose is tantamount to enslavement at worst; at best, it speaks to laziness and irresponsibility. The exercise of wise and godly followership is evident when prior to journeying, the follower determines that the leader's specific vision complements their general vision. Basically, general vision belongs to the follower and specific vision, the leader. For the follower and leader to exist in a harmonious relationship, their visions or desired outcomes must be complementary. In other words, it is the responsibility of the follower to ensure that his interests align with the objective of the potential leader. This truth is exemplified in the missional and evangelistic work of Christ, his Apostles, and Church. Jesus preached the message called the Gospel or Good News. The "goodness" of this message speaks to the great advantage and benefit offered to its recipients. In an oversimplified form, the message of Christ and his Church is this, "God is for you." His precise vision and detailed purpose for us is in perfect tandem with what we generally desire for our lives. Christ consistently taught his audiences they were pursuing death mistaking it for life. They were pursuing wretchedness believing it was wealth. They were pursuing enslavement convinced it was liberty. You see, the Gospel is God's specific vision for his creation, it is the complement to our General Vision. It presents in true and living color who we want to be and what we want to possess. Sin and Satan have so distorted our general vision of this glory that we unwittingly pursue a perversion. The Gospel is not only an invitation, it is an argument seeking to convince us that what we want and desperately need is consistent with what God desires and has for us. It calls us to examine with integrity the evidence presented. And upon conviction, to humbly, lovingly and unreservedly follow Jesus. This understanding and approach to faith in Christ can be applied to other areas of life, whenever there is a call or need to mobilize. The follower must weigh the evidence presented by a potential leader to ensure the existence of a complementary relationship between their general vision and the specific vision of the leader. If unconvinced, the wise thing to do is decline to follow.

Evaluate & Test

A third character trait of good followership is the ability to test or evaluate. Suppose someone has a clear awareness of their self and situation; and is convinced that they need help. Furthermore, they have happened upon a visionary whose detailed aspirations complement their general vision. Should they then follow this would-be leader? A harmony between specific and general vision does not automatically indicate the need to follow or the wisdom of trusting a person to lead us. We must also test and evaluate the character or credentials of the person we're considering following. When Moses argues with God against his commission to deliver Israel from Egyptian captivity, he asks God, "Who am I that I should go to Pharaoh and bring the children of Israel out of Egypt?" [Exodus 3.10-11]. Moses probably meant this as rhetorical question and was simply saying he was unworthy and of little significance. However, God takes the question literally and answers by assuring Moses of his continued presence. Additionally, God shores up Moses' resolve by giving him miraculous powers to serve as authenticating signs. God did not simply give Moses these assurances to boost his self-confidence or even his faith. God expected the people and elders of Israel to evaluate and test both Moses and his claims. These signs would serve to convince them that in their presence stood a man, whose specific vision not only complemented their general desire for freedom, but one who also possessed the ability to bring it about (Exodus 4.1-9 CSB). God expects us to do the same, evaluate for the authenticity of leadership before following. That God intends for his people to seek the authentication of would-be leaders is also affirmed in the case of Joshua, Moses' protege. Prior to Moses' passing, in accordance with

God's commands, he hands over the baton of leadership to Joshua (Numbers 27.18-23). The manner of Joshua's commissioning as ordered by God is both detailed and elaborate. The reason? So that the people of Israel would obey (*follow*) Joshua! Later on, God further authenticates Joshua's leadership with a powerful display of miraculous power (Joshua 3.7 - 4.14). We see these same occurrences in the life of Jesus. On more than one occasion, God authenticates Jesus as his son and the Messiah of Israel. This authentication finds its culmination in Jesus' resurrection from the dead (Acts 2.32-36). Thus, we can conclude that God expects his people to thoroughly evaluate and determine credibility before following anyone. Miraculous signs did not only confirm that these were people chosen by God for his children to follow. They also indicated that these people were leaders enabled by Him to accomplish the stated task. It should be noted that called and gifted leaders are not always authenticated with miraculous signs. The Bible is replete with numerous leaders such as Esther, Ezra and Nehemiah, who were called and gifted by God, but were not authenticated with mind-bending displays of supernatural power. The consistent marks of authentication we see in those called and gifted to lead are traits indicating reverence for God's words, ability and godly character. These people exhibit a deep knowledge and sincere love of God and his people. Finally, their lives must be consistent with the teachings of scripture. In other words, instead of looking for displays of the supernatural from potential leaders, we should evaluate and test the scriptural fidelity of their vision and character.

Simulsight

The follower's responsibility to evaluate must continue throughout their quest and relationship with any given leader. This is because people sometimes have character failings and remain unrepentant in such failed conditions. We see in scripture that leaders who fall in character and morality tend to suffer a loss in their ability to lead successfully. They tend to deviate from the original specific vision that was in harmony with the general vision of those following them. Scripture also shows that those who remain with such leaders share in their misfortune and fate. Therefore, it is the responsibility of followers, in the church and the wider culture, to know their leaders and to consistently have in their possession a clear handle on where they are being led. As we would for any other member of the church, we must befriend our leaders, love them and regularly check-in to ensure they are in prayer, studying and meditating on the Scriptures and walking in the Spirit. Simultaneously, we must also keep our eyes on the vision to ensure there is no deviation from the path no matter how slight.

Simulsight refers to the ability to simultaneously maintain focus on both the leader and his God-given specific vision for the community. Paul seems to capture this idea, when he tells the Corinthians to imitate him as he imitates Christ (1 Corinthians 11.1). Implicit in this instruction is the expectation that the Christians of Corinth are capable of simultaneously maintaining Paul and Jesus in their sights. Thus, the follower must constantly keep before them, the Vision Caster who in this case is Paul and the Vision, Christ. Followers must consistently evaluate the direction and character of the Caster against the Vision and what it demands of the community.

Simulsight affirms that even though God has given his people leaders, who are responsible to guide and care for them, he still expects them to look to him. In other words, the presence of church elders, comprising pastor, teachers and other leaders, does not shut the open access God's people have to their father in Heaven. An access we're instructed to consistently and unceasingly explore to the fullest (Philippians 4.6, 1Thessalonians 5.17; Hebrews 4.16, 1 Peter 5.7). As a matter of fact, failure to frequently enter such personal communion with God is tantamount to sin. John, the Apostle, hints at the reality of Simulsight and direct access when he tells his readers that they have an anointing from God (1John 2.20-27). John declares that this anointing teaches us all things. Furthermore, John states that he is telling us the truth, not because we don't know it, but because we do know it! We could erroneously interpret this passage to mean that Pastors and other Church Elders are unnecessary since we all have the Holy Spirit. That would be a grievous and dangerous mistake. After all, the very nature, tone and content of John's words are pastoral and educational in nature. So, what are we to make of this? I believe John is unearthing the concepts of Simulsight and General Vision. The Holy Spirit works through elders to teach, guide, protect and care for us. These leaders help clarify or expound truths we may already know. Many times, they challenge us to live out truths we may have never considered or turned away from. Other times, they teach us how to apply these truths in our daily lives. However, their work is consistently affirmed and testified to, by the very same Holy Spirit abiding and working within us. Thus, when a leader teaches or requires something new or unfamiliar, we are not to outrightly reject it, neither are we to welcome it with all-out excitement. On the contrary, we are too exercise restraint and seek the guiding and confirming witness of the Holy Scriptures and Spirit (Acts 17.11). Simulsight reminds Christians that they are all priests of God who have direct access to Him by the Holy Spirit through Jesus Christ. The reality of this intimate and living communion enables the follower to rely on the Caster for guidance and at the same time ensure they are on the right path. Simulsight helps us understand that followership is not passive business. It is neither for the timid nor lazy. Followers must always have their eyes wide open to observe, analyze and act. The humble and continuing work of holding our leaders accountable depends on the health of our Simulsight. Followers must make a discipline of both honoring our leaders by being pliable and immersing themselves in God through prayer and scripture study. Remember, Simulsight is the ability and process of simultaneously maintaining one's focus on both the one they are following and the place or person they are being led to.

Inquisitiveness

Inquisitiveness is the fifth element of good and godly followership. It is a natural corollary to Simulsight and an aspect of Evaluation. However, it is worth considering as an independent virtue because certain Christian communities actually discourage their members from this practice. Some are made to believe that they should accept the teachings and actions of their leaders without question. They are led to believe that questioning their leadership's teachings or decisions is tantamount to doubting God. Of course, such a position flies in the face of Jesus' questioning attitude. An attitude he possessed from childhood! (Luke 2.41-46) Furthermore, the call to love God with all our minds indicates his desire for us to think critically about what He says (Matthew 22.37, Isaiah 1.18).

It makes sense that our simultaneous focus on both Christ and those he has given to lead us (Simulsight) will yield perplexing discoveries. Some of these discoveries may be the character flaws or failings of our leaders and those within the Christian fellowship. They may be discoveries that reveal areas in which the church has erred and is erring. At other times, they may be findings that challenge us to trust God more. God does not intend for us to ignore these discoveries; instead we are to explore them. Inquisitiveness is a most essential quality of followership. We must explore and ask questions concerning the things we uncover. Provided our intentions are sincere, inquisitiveness will ensure our growth and act as a safeguard for our faith. By sincerity of intention, I mean that our inquiry should always be driven by the love of God and his people. Also, it should be characterized by a desire to preserve or grow the community in holiness and love. Godly inquisitiveness or inquiry must be carried out openly and constructively in humility. Followers should be aware that the spirit in which inquiries are made can actually lead to secrecy, discord and even destruction. Notice the conversation between the serpent and Eve begins with a simple inquiry, "Did God really say...?" (Genesis 3.1). One way to safeguard against such outcomes is to ensure that our questioning is not driven by a secret agenda. It would be wise and integrous to state in clear and simple language to one's self, the reason or origin of the inquiry, before posing it. Not only will this approach allow for the one being questioned to properly and fully address the inquiry, it will allow the inquirer to see the motivation of their heart.

Another benefit of inquiry is that it serves to foster sobriety and thoughtfulness. Leaders of communities in which inquiry is encouraged tend to exercise more thoughtfulness in their behavior. They are aware that they will have to give an account for their words and actions. Teaching and preaching are areas in which this is readily apparent. Pastors and preachers who allow for their congregants to question their sermon content find that they give more time and effort in study and preparation. In addition, such inquiry also encourages leaders because it signals that their community is actively engaged and interacting with the content of their messages. Beyond the pulpit, leaders can also be encouraged by inquisitive followers because it indicates those they serve, take them and their work seriously. Therefore, followers should not think their questions serve only to challenge or frustrate their God-given leaders. They should also realize that questioning, when done graciously, is a gift that encourages and inspires their leaders. Their inquiry indicates they are interacting with the leader's vision. By looking to him for answers, they affirm his call to serve the church. An affirmation of one's call is rarely ever unwelcomed. In times of testing, such affirming inquiry may be the life jacket that a leader desperately needs.

A Misplaced Priority

Loyalty

The scriptures recount an incident that occurred during Israel's wandering in the desert after their departure from Egypt (Numbers 11.25-29). In this episode, God takes from the spirit he has endued Moses with and places him on seventy men chosen to assist Moses in leading Israel. These men were presented to God in front of the tent that housed the Ark of the Covenant. The tribes of Israel camped around the tent of the ark but maintained a respectable distance from it. Thus, the general community was able to observe these men prophesying from a distance when God placed his spirit from Moses on them (Numbers 11.24-25). Scripture is silent on an explanation, but two of the seventy men remained within the community, that is, they were not presented before the tent. Nevertheless, God placed his Spirit on them as well and they began to prophesy. One can only imagine the wonder, excitement and maybe even fear that seized the camp. When a report of this incident was brought to Moses, Joshua, his aide de camp, responded by encouraging him to put a stop to it. Moses' reply reveals him to have been a very discerning man. He realized that his protégé was zealously protective of his position as leader and mouthpiece of God to Israel. Notice that Moses does not rebuff Joshua's support. All he does is correct Joshua's perception. Such jealousy and support for another can only be understood as loyalty.

Loyalty is strong and steady support or allegiance for another. It is an essential character of followership. It is also a quality that leaders desperately desire from those they lead. Understandably so, leaders face and fight a lot of resistance. It is so easy for them to feel alone and without help. People that support them through thick and thin are a priceless treasure. These people are a major source of comfort, enabling leaders to stay on task despite the various distractions they face. Often times, when leaders doubt their ability and calling, or the wisdom of their decisions, it is from these loyal followers they draw assurance and renewed strength. The ability to serve as a constant support for another will never be found among those who are weak and passive.

Loyalty is a trait that must never be exercised alone. Because, on its own, loyalty can be easily manipulated and misplaced. Many Christians have unwittingly hurt their brothers and sisters by remaining loyal to leaders, whose character and actions were brought into question. On occasion we have refrained from listening to those in our community when they expressed concerns about a leader. At other times, we have actively silenced and ridiculed them in a show of loyalty for an accused leader, only to discover that we were in error. It is important to understand that withholding support from a leader does not equate disloyalty nor does it mean that they are not cared for. There will be times, when our care and love for them actually demands the withdrawal of our support for them or their actions. Because of its delicate and powerful nature, we must jealously and consistently guard our tendency to loyalty with discernment and Simulsight. Discernment acts as a guard of loyalty, when it applies scripture in determining the process for testing and evaluating whatever statements or accusations are brought against our leaders. Basically, it ensures that we are justified in giving our firm and steady support to any leader.

On the other hand, Simulsight reminds us that our prime loyalty must always be to the vision and not the vision caster. The role Simulsight plays in ensuring one's loyalty is not misplaced, is captured in Matthew 16.21-23 and Mark 8.31-33. In this episode, we see Peter discouraging Jesus from accepting his passion and crucifixion. Mark simply tells us that Peter rebuked Christ for speaking of his impending ordeal. Matthew's account on the other hand, offers a little more detail. It reveals the very words Peter speaks, "Oh no, Lord! This will never happen to you!" Here we see that Peter's concern is primarily for Jesus' welfare. Compelled by a sense of intense loyalty, Peter unwittingly attempts to dissuade Christ from being faithful to his Father. Jesus' response confirms that though Peter's care and support is for him, that is for his human person, it is sorely misplaced. Peter's loyalty to Jesus was exempt of loyalty to the Father, "you're not thinking about God's concerns but human concerns." As a result, he becomes Satan personified! You see, Peter failed to salt his loyalty with simulsight. Many of us have followed Peter in this error. We have neglected to maintain a loyalty to our leaders that is in submission and harmony with loyalty to God. By doing this we have unknowingly become enemies of both God and the ones we sought to remain loyal to. Even worse, on countless occasions our misplaced loyalty has resulted in inflicting severe injury on other members of our community and family. Within the Christian community, our first and unshakeable loyalty must always be to Christ, our hope and glory. It is this loyalty to Christ that determines when and to what extent we should be loyal to others. No matter who they are, or how great their achievements, our neighborly loyalty must always be controlled by our loyalty to Jesus.

Submission

One last trait of godly and active followership is submission. This trait is also the most difficult to learn. Mastery of this trait requires that we continually acknowledge our lack and need of specific qualities that others possess. As some of these qualities are non-transferable, we must therefore continually affirm that we need others to get us where or what we desire. Submission is primarily an attitude, a settled posture of the heart and mind that is expressed in our act of compliance and imitation.

As Christians, we must understand that corporately, we constitute the community and family of God, the body and sole representative of Jesus Christ to creation. Individually, he has gifted and empowered us with differing and complementary abilities. To successfully achieve the work God has set before us, we must discern each other's divine abilities and work together. An essential part of laboring in discernment and unity is deferring to those gifted with the responsibility of caring, protecting and guiding us. Submission begins with our admittance of the fact that certain people have been gifted with the ability and responsibility of stewarding us. It is completed when we yield to their instructions and directives. By yield, I refer not to simply doing what they ask, but to welcoming their exercise of authority over us with gladness. In the Christian community, which is the family of God, it should be noted that such exercise of authority is exclusively for the purposes of nurturance and guidance. It is not an authority given for treading down or upon. Though, we have this kind of authority, it is reserved for exercise over serpents, scorpions, demons, principalities and spiritual powers (Luke 10.19 NASB). In other words, the authority and power to subjugate is given to the Christian for exercise over nature and spiritual wickedness in its various forms. Godly and wise followers are responsible to ensure no one treads upon them in the name of Christian leadership. Such is the nature of subjugation not submission. Subjugation is demanded and forcefully taken; submission is appealed for and joyfully given. Subjugation rest in the domain of conquerors; submission in the domain of shepherds and saviors. Sometimes the line separating subjugation from submission gets blurred. Many in the church have been deceived into subjugation through the erroneous and evil misinterpretation and application of scripture. One way to discern subjugation from submission is to determine whether the follower-leader dynamic is driven by fear or trust. Are you following the directives and instructions of a leader out of fear or out of trust? Do you follow them compelled by fear of loss, hurt or judgment? Or compelled by the certainty of their call, the sincerity of their love and the genuineness of their character? Is their joy and advantage to be found in the improvement of their lot or in your spiritual growth? Submission leaves power in the hand of the yielded. Subjugation strips all power and rights from the one yielded. A cursory look at both the incarnation and passion-crucifixion of Jesus reveal a relationship of submission, not subjugation. The Word willingly became flesh, even more became a servant. Jesus willingly submitted to the purposes of his father (John 1.14, Philippians 2.6-8). This indicates a voluntary participation on the part of the yielded in whatever the endeavor may be. Their willful participation affirms their possession of power and right. This becomes quite evident when Jesus boldly declares that his life was not to be stripped from him. Instead, he would sacrificially lay it down and powerfully take it up again, all for us (John 10.17-18). It cannot be any clearer, submission in the Christian community never equates a loss of entitlement or power to another. If you feel or think that you do not have a choice, any power or rights, beware you may be in a blissfully ignorant and dangerous state of subjugation. It should also be noted that the end of subjugation is sorrow and wretchedness. This stands in stark contrast to submission which offers the hope of real reward and glory (Philippians 2.8-11). Jesus' reception of reward from the Father serves as a model of our present state. We stand to reap the reward of guidance and nourishment when we submit to our godly leaders (Hebrews 13.17).

Questions (Principles of Godly Followership)

1. Share (or journal) about a time when self-awareness led you to follow someone.

2. Share (or journal) about a time when situational-awareness led you to follow someone.

3. Share (or journal) about a time when someone's specific vision complemented your general vision? Did you follow their lead? How did it turn out?

4. In the past, how have you evaluated and tested the character and vision of potential leaders?

5. What are some benefits of Simulsight?

6. In what ways does your church leadership encourage or discourage inquiry?

7. What can you do to ensure godly inquiry is encouraged in your church?

8. Have you or anyone you know suffered due to misplaced loyalty? How has it affected your relationship with the church?

9. What do you find difficult in submitting?

10. To what extent has the culture's perception of submission affected your willingness to submit?

11. Have you experienced or witnessed subjugation in a church? If so, what impressions did it leave on you?

CONCLUSION

It is possible that one may read this book and conclude that leadership and followership are mutually exclusive, that they are incompatible. You may feel the need to identify as either one or the other. This would be a grave mistake. Truth be told, no one is always leading nor always following. We may find ourselves in the position of followers at home but leading at work or school. We may find ourselves directing the way at home in a given moment but in the next relinquishing that responsibility to another. Followership and leadership are not binary; they are roles that require equal attention and proficiency for the effective functioning of any community or organization. Our present obsession with leadership has led to a failure to appreciate and develop followership as both a virtue and skill. A virtue because God made humans to be following creatures by nature and pronounced his creation to be good. Furthermore, we see followership modelled in Jesus' interaction with God and man. For the Christian there is no greater virtue than the imitation of Christ. In a number of instances, we find Jesus displaying followership in his dealings with many in the community. A few instances of Jesus compliance can be seen in, his departure from the temple for Nazareth at his parents beckoning (Luke 2.48-51), his turning water to wine at his mother's insistence (John 2.1-9), his payment of the temple tax in compliance with religious-traditional law (Matthew 17.24-27). On the other hand, followership is a skill because it can be learned and developed. We must learn, when to and when not to follow; how to and how not to follow; who to and who not to follow.

Our simultaneous appreciation of leadership and abandonment of followership can be likened to building a house without giving adequate attention to ensuring the soundness of its foundation. It would be no surprise if that house was to eventually topple over, as a matter it should be expected. If we do not correct our current course, we will find such a crumbling occur among our churches and the faith of many. This state of affairs can also be likened to a play that possesses great supporting roles and a very weak lead. Such a play ends up tepid, never reaching its fullest potential it leaves the audience completely dissatisfied. Despite the great emphasis we place on leaders and their part in the church, they are the supporting cast. The lead role is played by those who not only follow God but also follow those he has called to lead. The Christian community is a living body that works effectively when each individual part recognizes, rejoices and enthusiastically serves in their God-given and empowered role. This high level of cooperation and teamwork glorifies God and stands as a testimony to the world of his magnificent presence within the church. On the other hand, an unwillingness or inability to serve in one's role stands as evidence of disobedience or unfaithfulness. Both cases serve as an affront to God and offer the world justification for questioning the church's place as a giver of light. A renewed appreciation for the preeminence of followership and the pursuit of excellence in it will ensure that our work blesses both God and community.

My all-out quest to develop followership is not chiefly centered on the life of my children. I have primarily focused on growing my capacity to follow. I figure kids will be more prone to learn what they see practised in our lives. Thus far, I have learned a lot about followership. I will touch on two lessons that I found pleasantly surprising. Following is a joy, when one recognizes that it is a Christian virtue. There is a gladness of heart we experience when we follow the example of Jesus. Sometimes it is simply the joy we gain from knowing that Jesus is pleased with us. At other times, there is joy in the freedom of following because it is dissociated from weakness, passivity and foolishness. Understanding that following someone does not mean you're weak or foolish is liberating. It allows you connect with the deepest and most essential aspect of your nature without guilt or a sense of inferiority. Yes, God made you to follow and he declared you to be good. Finally, there is the exhilaration of embarking on an adventure. It allows you trust someone else to guide you to a destination you are not familiar with, on a path you most likely have not travelled before. Another surprising lesson I learned is that followership, when done correctly, tends to actually empower the follower! Gaining them the respect and admiration of their contemporaries. Often times, we find that different experiences in life tend to progress along paths that are similar in nature. As a result, we are able to apply lessons and skills acquired from prior experiences to successfully complete current projects and scale difficult present circumstances. It is the possession and application of these lessons and skills that garner the follower respect and admiration. These necessary skills and lessons, needed for our continued progress, are usually acquired from earlier experiences in which we learned to comply and imitate the examples of others. Simply put, the follower may be compared to a student who has mastered the skills they were taught. When such a student displays the skills they have acquired, they are often admired and regarded as experienced practitioners in their field. The same is true in the lives of those who follow wisely.

A Misplaced Priority

We live in a world that is desperately in need of movements capable of stemming the tide of corruption and wickedness we face daily. This wickedness and corruption finds expression in a plethora of forms, ranging from the murder and exploitation of the weak to the unchecked greed of the powerful. These movements for change comprise of leaders and followers. We do not suffer a shortage of leaders, instead we have so many leaders it's become difficult to differentiate the false from true, the inept from the adept. This state of affairs can only be allayed by recognizing followership as a virtue and discipline that must be acquired. Trained followers will be able to discern and empower true leaders. They will be keenly aware of their responsibility and take pride in their ability as followers.

The church of Jesus is at its best when complying with the commands and imitating the character of the Lord. This corporate ability to follow Jesus must first be present in the individual members who make up the community of faith. It is nourished and nurtured by our following of those among us gifted with leadership. Every successful venture of the church, at every point in history, was based on her compliance with and imitation of leaders empowered by Jesus the King. It is possible that when those in the world begin to follow because we follow, they may eventually come to know the one we follow. If, however, we continue on the path of an obsession with becoming leaders, we will not only prevent others from meeting Christ, we may find that we have given others license to determine their lives as opposed to looking to God. After all the desire to be the leader is ultimately a quest to satisfy our need to be the shot caller. Thus, we unintentionally say, do not look to Jesus, look to yourself instead.

It has been sometime since I discovered my allergic reaction to my son's followership tendencies. Upon looking back, I remember my instinct was to immediately say, "do not be a follower be a leader." Thank God for the gracious rebuke of his Spirit and scripture. Heather and I decided to work on developing followership in our kids. We encourage them to emulate what their friends say and do that is consistent with what we have taught them from the Bible. It hasn't been easy, they've been many times I have given in to the desire to push my children to be leaders, for leadership sake. They have been times when I felt disappointment at the ease with which they deferred to friends. Nonetheless, it has been an exciting journey. On several occasions I have overheard my children express disagreement with a particular decision even when they've had to stand alone. This has been most evident in my youngest, who rarely ever went against the grain. In learning to follow, he seems to have grasped the concept of good followership versus bad followership. We are not anti-leadership, as that would simply be an error in the opposite direction. Worse, it would be a neglection to produce in our kids a key aspect of Jesus' character. As a matter of fact, we now have a saying in our home that the kids repeat every morning when leaving for school, "follow the good, lead to the good." Leadership is great, however, it is founded and sustained by followership. In other words, it is important to make sure these disciplines are placed in the proper order. Nothing is gained when the cart is placed before the horse.

I pray that we come to a renewed appreciation of followership as the preeminent virtue and discipline for any truly effective and lasting movement. May this appreciation not obscure the importance and place of leadership. But by it, leadership will be better understood and exercised. There is no greater call than to follow Jesus, the God and creator of all things. May it be your sustenance and your joy.

Contact or Connect:

For over a decade, Ubi Ntewo has spoken at services, conferences and workshops all over the world. His passion is to clearly and faithfully teach God's word in the power of the Holy Spirit, making it applicable and relevant to his audiences. If you would like to have Ubi speak and teach at your event or to simply connect, please feel free to reach out.

 @UbiNtewo

 @UbisWork

EMAIL: created2follow@gmail.com

Made in the USA
Monee, IL
08 March 2021